D0521349

Discipleship Journal's Best Small-Group Ideas, Volume 2

Discipleship Journal's Best Small-Group Ideas, Volume 2

Compiled by Susan Nikaido

NAVPRESS®

BRINGING TRUTH TO LIFE

A Discipleship Journal® Book
Discipleship Journal® • P.O. Box 35004 • Colorado Springs, CO 80935
www.discipleshipjournal.com

The Navigators is an international Christian organization. Our mission is to advance the gospel of Jesus and His kingdom into the nations through spiritual generations of laborers living and discipling among the lost. We see a vital movement of the gospel, fueled by prevailing prayer, flowing freely through relational networks and out into the nations where workers for the kingdom are next door to everywhere.

NavPress is the publishing ministry of The Navigators. The mission of NavPress is to reach, disciple, and equip people to know Christ and make Him known by publishing life-related materials that are biblically rooted and culturally relevant. Our vision is to stimulate spiritual transformation through every product we publish.

ISBN 1-57683-848-X

Cover design by Adele Mulford
Creative Team: Susan Nikaido, Lori Mitchell, Laura Spray

Some of the anecdotal illustrations in this book are true to life and are included with the permission of the persons involved. All other illustrations are composites of real situations, and any resemblance to people living or dead is coincidental.

All Scripture quotations in this publication are taken from the HOLY BIBLE: NEW INTERNATIONAL VERSION® (NIV®), Copyright © 1973, 1978, 1984 by International Bible Society, used by permission of Zondervan Publishing House, all rights reserved; and the *New King James Version* (NKJV). Copyright © 1982 by Thomas Nelson, Inc. Used by permission. All rights reserved.

Discipleship journal's 101 best small-group ideas.
    p. cm.
    ISBN 0-89109-950-6 (pbk.)
    1. Church group work—Studying and teaching. 2. Small groups—Studying and teaching. I. Discipleship journal.
BV652.2.D57 1996   96—10263
253'.7—dc20   CIP

Printed in Canada

2 3 4 5 6 / 09 08 07 06

FOR A FREE CATALOG OF
NAVPRESS BOOKS & BIBLE STUDIES,
CALL 1-800-366-7788 (USA)
OR 1-800-839-4769 (CANADA)

Contents

Introduction

Psalm 68:6 says in part, "God sets the lonely in families." For me, God has fulfilled that promise through small groups.

Wherever I've lived, no matter what stage of life I've been in, I have sought out a small group to be a part of. Many of these groups have been like a family to me. They've prayed me through career decisions, dating struggles (and not-dating struggles), step-parenting dilemmas, and, most recently, a long and arduous adoption process.

Small groups have been a family to celebrate holidays with when I was far from home. They have given me a good laugh when I most needed it and a safe place to cry. Through small groups I've known the joy of being supported and cared for, and of supporting and caring for others.

What's more, by getting me into God's Word, small groups have kept me growing. As others share their stories and insights into Scripture, God speaks to me in ways that go beyond what I glean from time alone with my Bible. I've seen how small groups are often the setting in which we fulfill God's intention for us to accept one another (see Romans 15:7), encourage one another (see 1 Thessalonians 5:11), admonish one another (see Colossians 3:16), and above all, love one another (see 1 John 3:11). In the intimacy of a small group, I've experienced what it's like to have true brothers and sisters in Christ.

Unfortunately, however, some of my small groups have been more like dysfunctional families. In a group I started, one member began dominating the sharing time with her many problems, and the other members gradually quit coming. In another group, discussions never went beyond theological "right answers." I've also been frustrated by members who keep the door to their personal lives tightly closed, and by leaders who prefer expounding on their own insights to letting group members discover their own.

Just throwing a group of believers together in a room doesn't automatically create the kind of rich relationships we long for. Some will talk too much, others hardly at all. Prayer may get stuck at the surface level. Members may be uninterested in outreach. Bible study may become academic instead of life-changing. Even a group that's experiencing biblical fellowship can get into a rut.

This book is designed to help with the inevitable challenges of leading or being in a small group. It brings together the wisdom and creative ideas of dozens of small-group leaders who have contributed their best ideas for building dynamic groups. These ideas have passed the test in small groups like yours.

In the chapters that follow you'll find proven ways to help the Bible come alive, make prayer more meaningful, and build deeper relationships. You'll also find fresh ideas for evangelism, service, and involvement in missions. There's a chapter full of creative ways to celebrate holidays and seasons with your group. You'll also find principles every leader needs to know, as well as coaching on how to find and develop new small-group leaders.

Whether you need help with a difficult group member or a fresh way to approach your group prayer time, the ideas in this book can help your small group grow into the healthy, caring, growing family that God wants for each of us.

—Susan Nikaido

PART ONE

Small-Group Leaders

Best Ways to Plant, Water, and Grow Healthy Small Groups

3

Secrets of Small-Group Success

1
The Best Small-Group Leaders I've Known . . .

- *Loved God's Word.* It showed in the depth of their Bible study preparation and in their enthusiasm for talking about what they'd discovered. It also showed in their wise counsel based on scriptural truth.
- *Weren't afraid to flex.* These leaders would recognize it if we needed to spend the evening drawing strength from God in prayer instead of cranking through one more chapter of Bible study. If one person needed special love and encouragement, these leaders would value that person more highly than some prearranged schedule. They didn't allow chaos to reign—far from it—but people always took precedence over plans.
- *Were real people.* They didn't try to prove they were spiritual giants. They were honest about their flaws and struggles.
- *Modeled faithfulness.* They showed up week after week. Now that I lead small groups, I wonder how many times they wanted to spend the evening on the couch with a mindless video instead of guiding people through a convicting study of God's Word. Faithfulness counts.
- *Depended on God.* During our group prayer times, they would talk with God as if they knew Him intimately. Before the rest of us even arrived, they had bathed the evening in prayer. They knew who was really in charge of our growth.
- *Were creative.* The best leaders I've known made every week different in some small way. Maybe it was an icebreaker, the way they led into the study, the surprising use of music or communion, or just the challenging application questions they would ask.
- *Brought truth to life.* At the end of the evening, we had a clear sense of what that week's Scripture had to do with how we lived our lives. And there wasn't a pat answer to be found anywhere.

—SUE KLINE

2
What Mary Wants to Know

Mary has never attended a Bible study. You've just invited her to yours. But before she comes, she wants to know more than just the date, time, and place. She'll wonder:

- Will it be worth the time? Grocery lines and traffic jams consume Mary's precious extra minutes. She needs to know why a Bible study is a worthwhile time investment.
- Will it be relevant? Mary needs a "takeaway" after each session. She wants practical tools to implement Scripture into her life.
- Will the leader model genuine faith? Mary wants to get closer to Jesus. She is looking for someone to show her how.
- Will the material be too deep? New believers are turned off by long, theological discussions in "Biblespeak." They want the Scriptures to be presented in plain language.
- Will the material be too simple? Mary wants to grapple with life's tough issues, not "Bible Lite." She responds positively to a well-directed discussion and resents pat answers.
- Will I be put on the spot? Adults are embarrassed if called upon to speak or pray when they are not ready. They need assurance that they will not be asked to share prematurely.
- Will there be anyone like me? Mary is looking for fellowship. She wants to know she will fit in and be accepted by the group.
- Will the group do what it promises? Mary will become discouraged if she makes an effort to be on time and the group consistently starts late. She will be annoyed if she is the only one who reads the assigned material.
- Will they really care about me? A new member doesn't want to be just another body. Mary needs a pot of soup when she is sick and prayer before her job interview. She will feel loved when members remember her birthday and write to her kids at college.
- Will it be worth the effort? Adults have multiple responsibilities and packed schedules. Mary needs to hear you say, "This is the one hour of the week I wouldn't want to miss. If you come, I think you will feel that way, too."

—Kathy Widenhouse

3
Discussion Generators

Some leaders dominate their groups and are largely responsible for every word spoken. Imagine the difference if they would purposefully encourage discussion and create an environment where it can flourish! Here are a few ideas for helping you become a discussion-generating leader:

- *Ask open-ended questions.* Some questions slam the door on discussion—especially if they can be answered with a yes or no or a pat response. You get the expected answer, and then your group members sit there with a "what's next?" expression on their faces. A great question, however, unlocks the door to meaningful dialogue and interaction. It digs beneath the surface of superficial thinking. On a test, it would be an essay question as opposed to fill-in-the-blank. Practice your discussion questions on yourself. Do they beckon new discoveries?

  Good questions also keep your discussion going. "In what ways have you experienced this in your own life?" "What does this have to say to you, in the world you live in?" "What things do you find hard to accept about this?" "What difference would it make if this were not true?" With questions such as these, even pat answers open doors to deeper understanding.

- *Play devil's advocate.* Shake things up by arguing for the opposing view. State your case and challenge your group to prove you wrong. Christians often associate almost exclusively with those who agree with them. Awaken your group members' minds and deepen their beliefs by challenging their thinking in an environment where they can test their wings when the stakes aren't so high.

- *Prime the pump.* Get personal. Risk sharing a relevant experience from your own life—a struggle, victory, failure, piece of personal history. Others in the group will become more confident to open up if the leader is willing to drop the image of perfection and be honest. Let people know that this is a safe environment in which to share from the heart.

- *Cover the bases.* When a topic or passage is open to more than one interpretation, explain various dominant viewpoints. Your group will appreciate this a lot more than if you present your view as the only one in existence. State the options, but feel free to explain why you hold to the interpretation that you do. Then encourage discussion of the strengths and weaknesses of the competing viewpoints.

—John Green

4
Leadership Unmasked

Too often, I find myself tempted to wear my "perfect Christian" mask as I lead my small group. Yet my friends respond best when I am authentic. Here are some ways you can remind yourself to take off your own mask and enjoy genuine intimacy with your group members.

- *Be transparent in prayer.* Instead of sterile prayers, I've learned to pray honest, humble prayers where I confess my neediness before God and group members. They see it's not bad to be needy as long as we remember God is there to meet our needs.

- *Admit sin struggles.* One day when leading a group of new Christians, I admitted a sin I was battling. "I didn't know you still sinned," one of the women said, amazed. She and the others were comforted to realize that my relationship with God is strong though I struggle with sin as they do.

- *Use examples from your life.* So many times I've thought, "If I tell them one more thing about my shortcomings, surely they'll quit this group." Instead, my transparency draws us closer and encourages others to open up.

- *Ask for help.* Often we can wear a mask of self-sufficiency and think we have come only to serve and never to be served. Recently I asked a group member to help me organize my home office. I also ask for help each time I inquire, "Will you please pray for me?"

- *Learn to say, "I don't know."* I used to feel I was a lousy leader if I didn't know an answer. Now I've learned to say, "That's a good question, but I don't really know." That opens the floor to others, and together we search for answers.

- *Show emotion.* When something sad has happened to me, I've been tempted to hide my pain. How freeing it is to share my heartache and occasionally let tears flow. This has drawn our group closer as we learn to "mourn with those who mourn" (Romans 12:15).

- *Point to God's faithfulness.* The purpose of removing our masks is not to demonstrate our sinfulness but to demonstrate God's faithfulness. Transparency reminds group members that any holiness in me is simply the result of God's continuing work in my life. I emphasize that He wants to do the same for them.

—ELAINE CREASMAN

5
Growing Closer When You're Apart

No matter what I did to make our meetings dynamic, it didn't guarantee people would attend or interact. But then I discovered that whenever I made a midweek connection with a group member, he was sure to attend and participate in our next meeting. Here are some things my wife and I have done to help our group grow closer when we're apart.

- *Visit them at work.* I'm interested in what people do for a living—and people are usually eager to show me this part of their lives. I ask when is the best time for me to visit them at work, so they can show me around. When I show interest in their work, people seem more willing to share other parts of their lives as well.
- *Socialize with them.* It's often while playing and laughing together that we let our guard down and allow our real selves to come out. Play sports together. Attend a retreat. Go to a concert. Camp overnight. Take a day hike. Play laser tag.
- *Serve them.* There are obvious times when people need help—during illness or when facing a big move, for example. But don't overlook opportunities to be kind in small ways as well. My wife sometimes offers to babysit so that young mothers in our group have time to be alone, go shopping, and so on.
- *Write them.* Personal, handwritten notes are becoming a rarity—and thus precious. I do four things to make the most of my notes to group members. I pray for God to guide my words. I focus on encouragement. I include a verse of Scripture. I tell them I have prayed for them.

- *Call them.* Many times my wife calls other women in our group just to connect briefly—and to have a sane adult conversation after hours of constant dialoguing with children. Casual phone calls communicate, "You're my friend."
- *Intercede for them.* A key to effective intercession is to identify with those for whom we pray. What's going on in their lives? Are they lonely? Stressed out with parenting? Struggling in a shaky marriage? Tempted at work to do something unethical? Put yourself in their place as you pray.

—BRIAN MAVIS

6
Happy Endings

Few small groups go on forever. When the time comes for your group to end, the following tips will help you finish well.

- *Remember the past.* Take time to retell ways in which Christ worked in your lives through your small group, such as answered prayers, transformed attitudes, or an increased understanding of the Bible. What was the happiest moment in the group? When did you laugh the most? What challenges did you overcome?
- *Release people to future ministry.* Celebrate future plans for ministry—to form another small group, to get more involved in the community, to volunteer at church, to move to a mission field, and so on. Reinforce that the end of your small group is not the end of personal and ministry growth.
- *Acknowledge accomplishments.* Reminisce with your group about what you've accomplished together—studies completed, outreach projects, relationship-building events—and give one another some well-deserved applause.
- *Evaluate.* If you spend time discussing the good and bad of your group experience, you will leave with a clearer idea of what you want your next small group to be like. Was your group caring? Loving? Was the curriculum too challenging or too easy? Look at your group covenant: Did you accomplish the goals and objectives you set as a group?
- *End with a bang.* Don't end your group without a party. Perhaps you'd

like to create personal collages at your celebration. Provide glue and poster or construction paper—one sheet per group member. Ask people ahead of time to bring cutouts from magazines or newspapers that remind them of fellow group members—ideally, at least two cutouts for each member. After you present each other with the images you've chosen (and explanations!), it's time to make collages. Each person makes his own collage by pasting the images people have given him to poster paper. Everyone leaves the party with a collage of memories.

At the end of the celebration, close with prayer for one another. Ask group members to complete the prayer sentence, "I ask that God grant you . . ." One of my former small groups sealed our time together with a communion service I will never forget. We had a happy ending. So can you.

—Murphy Belding

Sticky Situations

7
Chatty Cathy
and Silent Sal

Every group has them—the people who like to talk and the people who are happy to let them! Silent members can perplex and frustrate talkative group members and even leaders. Here are some thoughts on how to handle your subdued group members from two perspectives: a confessed quiet member and her more talkative counterpart.

Silent Sal Speaks

"When I'm silent, I'm usually thinking about the study, what others are saying, and what I think. Sometimes, I may feel uncomfortable speaking up—for a variety of reasons. Never put me on the spot! Warn me, outside the group setting, before you ask me to speak. After you've investigated privately why I'm quiet, ask me to help you discover a way to involve me in the discussion.

"To begin with, you can slow down the pace. Often, just about the time I'm ready to speak, either a talkative person speaks again or you move on to the next question. When you feel the pressure of silence, stop and silently count to 10. When the silence hangs there just a few moments, that's about the time I'm ready to speak up. If you force me to speak rather than using kindness to draw me in, I may disappear from the group altogether."

Chatty Cathy Speaks

"I get uncomfortable with silence for several reasons. I usually assume you want my help with the discussion, so my urge is to jump in to get things going. Often, I go home feeling as if I dominated the entire discussion.

"Talk to me privately if you think I'm talking too much. Maybe my role is to be an encourager instead. If I tell the quiet ones privately how much I value their opinion, and if I count to 10 before I enter the discussion, our roles may reverse. I may learn to enjoy listening!"

—Dianne E. Butts and Betty J. Johnson

8
When Someone Arrives in Pain

We had all settled in with our coffee, ready to begin our Bible study. But it soon became obvious that one group member was fighting back tears. So we stopped and said, "We'd like to listen if you want to talk." The floodgates opened, and we spent the next half hour ministering to this woman.

Small-group ministry includes bearing one another's burdens. Here are some considerations for the next time someone comes to your group in pain.

- If possible, acknowledge the person's pain privately before your meeting and ask her if she wants to let the group know what's going on. If not, keep it confidential.
- Remember that this situation is not a surprise to God. He is in control of the situation and the group.
- Ideally, your group will have discussed in advance how to respond to people in pain. Members will know not to jump in immediately with well-meant advice. Instead, they will gently ask questions and draw out the hurting person. They'll be discerning in what they share about their own experiences—no horror stories, but only those personal accounts that communicate empathy.
- If certain verses come to mind, jot them on a piece of paper and give them to the person later. It is usually best not to quote Scripture while a person is pouring out his pain.
- Spend a few minutes in prayer. Incorporate the power of touch by holding hands or laying hands on the person in pain.
- When you sense the person is finished sharing, take a coffee break to decompress and then return to the lesson.
- Before you leave, ask how the group can help. Make a plan for ongoing, practical support. If the response is, "Just pray for me," do it, then check back in a day or two.
- Make sure the whole group knows and understands these principles.

—Marsha Crockett

9
Problem People

The groan was almost audible as Sue (not her real name) verbally slammed her husband during our Bible study. The group was growing tired of her inappropriate and off-color comments, and the attitude toward her was worsening weekly.

We all encounter people similar to Sue: vocal people who make us cringe inwardly whenever they open their mouths, rough-around-the-edges people who offend us, opinionated people who make us roll our eyes in exasperation, unlovely people we'd rather avoid.

Some of these people end up in our small groups. How can we replace the groan in our hearts with Christ's love? Here are some steps I've found helpful.

- *Recognize Jesus' love for them* (see Matthew 9:12).
- *View myself accurately*—as equally needy before God (see Romans 3:23).
- *Do a heart check.* Perhaps the problem isn't them, but my own attitude (see Matthew 7:1-5).
- *Befriend them.* We often judge or criticize people without knowing much about them. Finding out that Sue had attention deficit hyperactivity disorder helped me understand her impulsiveness as a medical issue as well as one of self-control. It increased my compassion for her.
- *Stop commiserating with others about how inappropriate or problematic that person is.* Gossip only compounds the problem (see Proverbs 26:20).
- *Model grace.* As I learned to respond graciously to Sue, others seemed to follow suit, and the atmosphere of our small group changed dramatically.
- *Disciple them.* Offer to meet with them for a set period of time to work on a specific area of needed growth or study. Developing a relationship with Sue convinced her of my love for her. When we looked together at Ephesians 4:29 and discussed the issue of unwholesome versus helpful talk, she received the correction in the spirit intended. As I met with Sue, she became a more positive and welcome contributor in our small group.
- *Pray for them*—not just during your quiet time but during your meeting as they speak. Also pray with them outside of meeting times.
- *Expect the best.* Look for evidence of growth, and affirm the positive. Trust God to grow them (see 2 Corinthians 5:17; Ephesians 3:20; Philippians 1:6).

As I've practiced these principles, Sue has become a blessing to my heart and to our entire small group. Hidden beneath her rough edges was a woman truly after God's own heart. Imagine what we would have missed if I hadn't listened to the voice of God prompting me to love her.

—Joan Esherick

10
Banish the Blahs

Sooner or later, it happens to every group. You're moving along just fine—and then the blahs strike. The people in your group bore you. Scripture is dry as dust. Your prayers all land in the ceiling corner with the cobwebs.

If the blahs linger, people start dropping out of the group. What can you do? In his book, *Real Small Groups Don't Just Happen*, Neal McBride suggests these blah busters. Try one or two in your group.

- *Suspend your usual format or agenda for two or three weeks, and do something entirely different.* Brainstorm by asking group members, "What is something you've always wanted to do with this group?"
- *Go on a weekend retreat.* Escape as a group for fun and relaxation.
- *Change your setting by switching to a new location.* If you've been meeting at the church, meet in a home. If you're tired of meeting in homes, meet at a restaurant. If weather permits, meet outdoors.
- *Tackle a worthwhile project together.* Commit to helping every Saturday for a month at a homeless shelter. Or volunteer as a group to staff the church nursery.
- *In extreme cases, take a month off.* Sometimes absence does make the heart grow fonder.
- *Meet with another group for several weeks.* Study a particular topic together or watch and discuss a video series.
- *Switch how you learn.* If you've always done Bible studies, try a video series or a book. If you've always studied books of the Bible, try doing a topical study or character study.

—Sue Kline

11
What About the Children?

Include the children, or not? Provide activities for them in another room of the house, or not? Small groups consisting of young couples often face such questions. Some groups opt for a "no children except nursing babies" policy. This can work if everyone has access to a trusted babysitter and can afford the expense. Many young couples, however, are struggling financially.

If your small group is wondering, "What do we do with the kids?" here are some solutions to consider.

- *Hire a babysitter for the entire group.* She can keep the children in another room or at a nearby house. The entire group chips in to pay her. She could just babysit or provide spiritually nurturing activities for the children.
- *Ask group members to rotate as babysitters.* This can only work if everyone commits to take a turn. The advantage is that all the adults build relationships with all the children. The disadvantage is that someone misses the meeting.
- *Couples swap children with couples from another small group that meets on a different night.* The Smiths watch the Johnson children when the Johnsons go to small group on Tuesday. On Thursday, the Johnsons watch the Smith children so the Smiths can attend their small group.
- *Children participate for part of the meeting.* They could join in for singing or icebreakers. For the rest of the time, they might watch a video in another room with an adult or teen supervising.
- *Children stay for the entire meeting.* Older children can fully participate, and the younger ones can color or read picture books. This requires that your meetings offer something for all age levels.

—MEREDITH CURTIS

Training New Leaders

12
Discovering New Leaders

A small group is the ideal place to develop future leaders, not simply long-time followers. As the current leader, you're in a position to identify small-group members who are ripe to lead. Be deliberate about your search for new leaders. As you meet with your group, watch for God to spotlight the special qualities He has placed in each person. And ask yourself some of the following questions:

- Which member of the group openly shares how she applies Scripture to her life?
- Who takes notes or asks for clarification?
- Which person would I feel comfortable calling on to present a short devotional talk next week?
- Which member consistently reaches out in love to the others in the group?
- Who shares her creative abilities with the rest of the group?
- Who looks for ways to make the group successful?
- Who stands out in my mind as gladly sacrificing her time, talent, and treasure in serving the Lord?
- Who gives freely without requiring acknowledgment?
- Who is teachable, flexible, and eager to try new things?
- When presented with a new idea, who listens and discusses it instead of arguing for the way things have always been done?
- Finally, is there someone God might be pointing out as a potential leader who seems an unlikely choice to me?

—Cathy Miller

13
How to Encourage Reluctant Leaders

Many times, we sense certain members are ready to lead their own groups, but their fears keep them from taking that step. Here are some ideas for addressing the concerns of potential leaders.

- *I don't have enough talent.* Point out leadership qualities you've observed. Remind the potential leader that motives are more important than developed talent. Suggest using a Bible study with a leader's guide to help with lesson planning.

- *I don't know how to start.* Pray together, and remind him prayer is the best start. Suggest he start inviting people one at a time as the Lord brings them to mind. Rehearse how he might approach prospective members.

- *I don't know what to say.* Describe how you prepare. Show him the resources you use. Stress the value of planning the lessons ahead and jotting down what to say. Remind him that sometimes the toughest questions lead to the best discussions.

- *You're better than I'll ever be.* God doesn't want carbon copies; He wants willing servants. Write a letter to your reluctant leader, expressing reasons you believe the person will do well.

- *What if we get into a heated discussion?* Share your best methods for keeping on track and cooling down controversies.

- *I might be awful.* We often learn more from failure than success. Furthermore, it takes a whole group to succeed, so encourage the potential leader not to shoulder all the blame in difficult times. Let him know you're available to listen, share concerns, or give advice.

- *People may criticize.* Relate how you've learned to forgive those who criticize and accept constructive criticism as an opportunity for improving.

—Karen H. Whiting

14
Mentoring New Leaders

When I asked several small-group leaders what their worst fears were when they led for the first time, here's what I heard: "Feeling inadequate." "That no one would come." "I'll be boring." "My mind will go blank." "I don't know enough."

Here are some tips for easing anxiety and adding encouragement as you mentor those new to small-group leadership.

Do

- Lay aside perfectionism and unrealistic expectations. Acknowledge that leadership development is a process, not a state of perfection.
- Share (and laugh about) your own early experiences in leadership and how God used them to help you grow. Diffuse anxiety by being vulnerable about the mistakes you made along the way.
- Let others see your commitment to the new leader by praising her in front of her peers.
- Call her and send encouraging notes. Look for creative ways to encourage and build her up, giving her assurance that she's not alone.
- Communicate clearly, openly, and honestly. Truth spoken in love is a gift we can offer potential leaders.
- Establish healthy boundaries. You might want to agree not to phone each other on weekends or after a certain hour in the evening. This will help you respect each other's personal lives.

Don't

- Try to make her into another you. Instead, focus on her uniqueness, knowing that God will use her personality, temperament, gifts, and talents for His own purposes.
- Hold on too tightly. Give her room to make mistakes, so she will learn by doing and have the freedom to be creative.
- Inadvertently set her up to fail by offering opportunities that don't allow her to use her spiritual gifts, giving her insufficient time to prepare, or leaving her on her own the first time she serves.
- Infringe on her family time. Set the example of putting family before ministry, and encourage her to do the same.
- Finally, don't forget that God is using you to bless her . . . for His name's sake.

—CATHY MILLER

PART TWO

Small-Group Ideas

Hands-On Ideas for Immediate Use in Small Groups

Bible Study

Bible Study Basics: Principles for Understanding and Applying God's Word

15
Those Difficult Passages

You're preparing your Bible study, and there it is: a difficult passage. You read and reread, grappling with the question: What exactly is this passage saying? And if you are wrestling with a passage, the other small-group members are sure to be, too.

What do you do when a passage's meaning remains elusive? And if you're a group leader, how do you help those you lead to overcome their fear of difficult passages and to decipher them appropriately?

- *Pray.* Ask God to show you wonderful things in His Word.
- *Cross-reference.* Allow Scripture to interpret Scripture. Find other passages that speak to this issue. What clarification do they offer?
- *Examine the context.* The surrounding verses help determine the meaning of a passage. Search them for clues to the difficult verse's meaning.
- *Check commentaries.* Be selective and knowledgeable about available reference materials. Your pastor can recommend solid commentaries that will help you. Be willing to examine all sides of a controversial passage.

  One resource I have found helpful when dealing with difficult passages is *Encyclopedia of Bible Difficulties* by Gleason L. Archer (Zondervan). Categorized by books of the Bible, it includes a section called "Recommended Procedures in Dealing with Bible Difficulties."
- *Depend on the Holy Spirit.* He is your teacher and the Spirit of truth (see Luke 12:12; John 15:26).
- *Use your time wisely.* Don't spend an inordinate amount of time on a troublesome verse or two. You'll miss the clear teaching in the rest of the study. Some Scriptures may remain a mystery this side of heaven. Acknowledge that and move on.

—Beth K. Vogt

16
Navigation Tips for New Believers

New believers hunger to know God's Word, but there's so much to learn, and they don't know what to read first. When new Christians join your small group, you can help them navigate their Bibles and inspire them to read more.

- *Ask the new member to arrive early or stay late.* Go over her Bible's table of contents, introduce her to the types of books, and examine any special features of her Bible, such as a concordance.
- *Distribute bookmarks with the names of the books of the Bible in order.* On the reverse side, print the books in alphabetical order with symbols next to them indicating Old or New Testament and type of book—historical, prophet, gospel, and so on.
- *Give extra information when citing a verse.* Say, "Let's look at a verse in the book of Ruth, an Old Testament historical book, located after Judges and before 1 Samuel."
- *Use a CD-Bible or free Internet Bible site* (such as http://bible.gospelcom. net) to print out the verses before meetings. Give group members copies so that they can read along, and suggest that they locate each verse in their Bibles once they get home.
- *Before meetings, write Bible references on slips of paper that you place in a basket.* As members arrive, ask each to grab a paper and find the assigned verse. Ask people to read their verses at the appropriate time.

—Karen Whiting

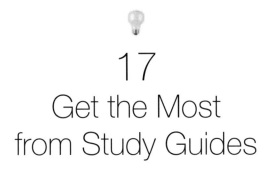

17
Get the Most from Study Guides

With the abundance of Bible study guides available today, how do you know which to choose? And how do you get the most benefit from them? Here are several tips to guide you as you choose and use a study guide.

Before You Choose

- Consider the style. Ask yourself, Is this a fill-in-the-blank guide that will help my group gain basic knowledge? Or are the questions more open-ended and designed as discussion starters and thought provokers? Will these questions help us reach greater personal insight and life change?
- Consider the leadership requirements. How much leadership is required to keep the lesson going? Are there tips for leaders? Can the book be used in a variety of ways? How will the lesson be affected if some have not studied ahead of time?

As You Participate

Share these guidelines with your group members.

- Look at the study guide as a way for God to speak to you rather than a homework paper to fill in at the last minute.
- Read ahead before writing your answers to get an overview of how the lesson will develop.
- Highlight phrases or words you don't understand. Underline or note the ideas you want to discuss further. Read the assigned Scriptures.
- Pace yourself. Complete enough of the study each day so you'll be done by the meeting.
- Ask yourself afterward: Which questions and Scriptures really spoke to me and why? What action or attitude will I ask Christ to change in me this week?

—Marsha Crockett

18
Applications That Stick

Does this scenario sound familiar? A leader finishes the lesson with, "How can we apply this?" Group members take a moment to reflect, then cautiously respond: "Well, maybe I could be more patient with my kids," or "I need to stop spending so much money." The group members then pray for grace to apply what they've learned and leave full of hopeful resolve to change. Next week the group returns, but resolve has given way to discouragement over failure to apply last week's lesson.

Our failure to successfully live what we've learned is often the result of misunderstanding how to apply truth. To help your members avoid this sense of failure, make sure your lesson applications are

- *Specific.* Take prayer, for example. "I need to pray more" may sound like good application, but it's too vague. A better plan would be, "I will set aside 10 minutes a day, five days a week, for focused prayer."
- *Realistic.* Let's say my small-group study challenges me to spend more time in God's Word. A resolution to get up every morning at four and spend two hours studying the Bible is unrealistic and sets me up for failure. A more realistic application might be, "I will read one chapter of Proverbs a day for the next 31 days."
- *Measurable.* Effective application will answer the question, How will I know I've successfully applied this truth? "I need to affirm my kids more" is vague. But "at least once a day, I will thank each child for one good thing he or she does" can be measured. By the end of the day, either I thanked them or I didn't.
- *Short term and long term.* When my husband and I became convinced we needed to be better stewards of our finances, we set short-term goals such as "keep a daily record of cash spent" and long-term goals such as "attend a financial management seminar this year." The short and long term together provided an avenue for continued application over time.
- *Flexible.* Several years ago, I was convicted of the need to study Scripture more regularly. I applied this by studying while my kids were at school. But when I needed to home school my son after an illness, I had to adjust the application.
- *Periodically reviewed.* Regular review (every three or six months) helps us examine how we're doing and adjust course as necessary.

—Joan Esherick

Bible Study

Fresh Ideas: Creative Approaches
to Topics and Passages

19
An Eyewitness Journal: The Gospels

In the course of regular devotional reading and Bible study, we can begin to view the characters as fictional. This prevents us from grasping the reality and application of the stories. One cure is to compile an eyewitness journal. The goal is twofold. First, to see oneself in the story so that Christ's ministry can be experienced afresh. Second, to imagine the thoughts, emotions, and reactions of the disciples, who, like us, were very human.

While studying one of the gospels, have your group members rewrite each episode involving Jesus and His disciples in first-person, present tense form. For example, from Matthew 8, a group member may write:

We almost drowned today! While we were on the lake, a fierce storm blew up. I was terrified! I was also a little angry, because Jesus was sound asleep in the boat. Didn't He care about us? We woke Him, and to my relief (and amazement) He stopped the storm. Then He scolded us for our lack of faith! Here we are, struggling to stay alive, and He lectures us! I guess He's trying to help us understand His power, provision, and love.

When your group meets, invite everyone to read their journal entries, then discuss the contemporary application. From Matthew 8, for example, you might ask, "What storm are you presently experiencing? How do you perceive Jesus as reacting to your dilemma? Why do we try to battle storms in our own strength?"

—MATTHEW WILLMINGTON

20
You Are There: The Gospels

When our adult small group was going through the Gospel of John, I tried to think of fresh ways to teach familiar passages. When we got to John 18, I wanted to help people imagine themselves at the arrest and trial of Jesus.

We meet in my house, so before people arrived, I labeled each room as a location in the story (the upper room, Gethsemane, Pilate's palace, Caiaphas' house, and so forth).

As people arrived, I gave them a printed copy of the passage and assigned them a role to play. Then we read the passage as we moved from room to room, according to where the story took us. We even turned out the lights and used flashlights for the night scenes.

The discussion that followed was fresher and livelier than it had been for some time.

—Gary Cantwell

21
Be Still: Quiet Time

In our small group, we had been stressing the importance of practicing a daily quiet time. One week we decided to have a "silent meeting" to demonstrate the benefit of being still before the Lord.

As group members arrived, we gave each one an agenda describing the segments of the evening.

The first 30 minutes were for prayer. The room lights were dimmed. Some chose to kneel, some sat on the couch, and some reclined on the floor to pray silently.

The next 15 minutes were for Scripture reading. We were to read to ourselves for a while and then select a passage of particular significance. Later, we could share these verses with the group if we wanted to do so.

The final 15 minutes were spent listening as a few people played guitars. (During our next silent meeting we might add communion to this segment.)

To close the evening, we took turns sharing our Scripture passages and what they meant to us, as well as our thoughts about the night. Though most confessed that it was difficult being quiet in a group of people, all agreed it was one of our most meaningful meetings. Some commented that it had been hard to establish a quiet time at home (the enemy of our souls sees to that), but they now had a renewed determination.

In our hurried lives, and sometimes hurried church services, we often talk, sing, and learn about God. It was nice to be still and be with God.

—Cydney Haynes

22
Treasure Hunt: Seeking God

It was Heart Group time at a Christian growth center for women addicted to alcohol, drugs, or prostitution. The topic was seeking God. I asked Him to show me how to convey this biblical concept to these women. The idea came to me to hide small amounts of money in the room.

Once all the women had arrived, I told them they had five minutes to search for hidden treasure. They could keep whatever they retrieved. After giving them the "Go!" signal, I observed their varied reactions.

Lily was off and running, literally turning the room upside down. Quarters, dimes, nickels, pennies, and a crumpled dollar bill inside the colored foil of a blooming poinsettia—she found them all.

Teri started out "hot," but her efforts were superficial, yielding only a dime or two.

Satisfied with 65¢ for the soda machine, Helen announced, "I quit."

Tina joined the hunt only when asked to look under the sofa cushion where she sat. She pocketed her first and only quarter.

Others hadn't even begun to search when I called, "Time!"

A lively discussion followed our treasure hunt. Each group member evaluated what kind of seeker she had proved to be. We then looked at what Scripture had to say about seeking God, and formulated the following principles.

- Seeking God is a commitment (see 2 Chronicles 15:12; Psalm 27:8).
- Seek wholeheartedly (see Deuteronomy 4:29).
- Make seeking a priority (see Matthew 6:33).
- Don't quit seeking (see Psalm 105:4).
- Believe God's promise that you will find Him (see 2 Chronicles 7:14; Proverbs 8:17; Jeremiah 29:13).
- Seeking brings rewards (see Hebrews 11:6).
- Seek now; time is limited (see Isaiah 55:6).

I am confident that whenever these women encounter a verse about seeking God, they will remember our treasure hunt and the insights we all uncovered.

—BLANCHE GOSSELIN

23
No Unimportant Pieces: The Body of Christ

The next time you would like to emphasize to your small group the concept of "one body, many parts" (1 Corinthians 12), try this activity. Purchase a children's jigsaw puzzle that has approximately the same number of pieces as you have group members. Mail one piece to each person, with instructions to bring that piece to the next meeting.

As people arrive, ask them to place their pieces into the puzzle. When it's time to start your study, examine the puzzle together. Are all the pieces in place? This is a beautiful picture of the oneness of the body of Christ. Each part contributes to the whole. Each part connects to the others and keeps them from slipping away.

Are pieces missing? That's a powerful illustration of how the body of Christ is incomplete if one of us fails to use his or her gifts and to maintain fellowship with the rest. The picture becomes marred. Even the pieces that "showed up" may be isolated and unattached, making them more prone to fall out of the picture altogether.

Whether your puzzle ends up fully assembled or not, you've given your group members a fresh way to visualize their importance, even if they only feel like a small piece of God's puzzle.

—Carol R. Cool

24
A Stone's Throw: Worry

If you've been studying trusting God or handling worry and anxiety, this activity can drive home the message. I've done this at exam time for students, when stress levels are high. Take your group to a pond or lake (check in advance to make sure there are plenty of small rocks along the shoreline). Give people felt-tip markers.

Tell them to grab some stones and write on each a word or phrase that describes what they are anxious about. Then, while screaming your heads off, throw your stones into the lake. After the hilarity settles down, take turns reading appropriate verses about peace, burdens, anxiety, and related topics.

—MILLIE WELSH

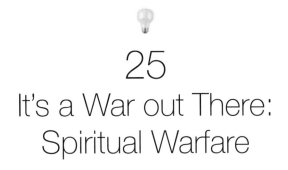

25
It's a War out There: Spiritual Warfare

Our home group is studying spiritual warfare. To help us visualize what warfare is like, the men in our group went to see the movie *Black Hawk Down*. Afterward, we sat over coffee and compared and contrasted the military warfare we had just seen with spiritual warfare. We came up with more than 40 observations. (Caution: The movie is rated R for violence.)

Black Hawk Down is just one of many war movies that would work for this exercise. Check out local movie listings or your local video rental store.

—DEREK D. HEE

26
Lights Out!: 1 John 1:1-7

For one of our Bible studies, we darkened the room before group members arrived. They had to find a place to sit in the dark. Once people were in place, we lit a match, then a flashlight, and finally a lamp.

It was interesting to talk about our reactions: Some people were scared at first. We all felt much better when the match was lit, and better still with the lamp.

Next, we talked about our lesson from 1 John 1:1-7: walking in darkness. We observed that we eventually get comfortable in the dark. And it's easier to tolerate the dark if others are in the dark with us. We also discussed all the things you cannot see in the dark. Thanks to our experiment, we gained deeper insight into living in the light.

—Sean Michael Murphy

27
Small-Group Psalmnody: Thankfulness

To cultivate thankfulness among your group members, take a look at the ancient yet effective method found in Psalm 136. In this psalm, which recounts God's mighty acts on Israel's behalf, each verse is followed by the refrain "*His love endures forever.*"

Your group can write its own version of Psalm 136, using the original as a pattern.

- Read the psalm aloud, or ask members to read silently. Explain that verses one to three encourage thanks for God Himself; four to nine for His acts in creation. The rest of the poem cites ways He cared for Israel.
- Ask members to write down one way God worked to bring them to faith in Christ, using verses 10 to 25 as a guide. Point out themes in the original: God's deliverance, intercession, provision, defeat of Satan, and gift of a new life.
- Choose a narrator to lead in a responsive reading of verses one to nine. Group members repeat the refrain after each verse. Next, ask members to read what they've written. They may say things such as "I thank God who allowed me to go broke so I'd reach out to Him."
- After each, the group responds, "His love endures forever." Close with verse 26.

Through this activity, your group will create a corporate, capsulated history of God's goodness. Repeat the process on other occasions with fresh reasons to praise, including the ways God has blessed your church and families, helped during trials, or deepened relationships with Him.

Urge members to use this pattern for praise by writing a personal version in their private worship. In the small group, with families, or alone, this can be a powerful reminder that God's love indeed endures forever.

—Marion Duckworth

28
Playing with Paste: The Beatitudes

Who says crafts are just for kids? I tried this with my adult small group and they loved it—including the men!

For our study on the Beatitudes, I brought in plain white paper, scissors, glue, stickers, crayons, markers, and lots of words and pictures cut from magazines. I assigned each person (or couple) a beatitude and gave them 10 minutes to create a picture of their verse. Then we displayed the results and tried to guess which beatitude was represented by each picture.

An alternative is to give group members an 8 1/2" by 11" piece of paper folded into eight squares and ask them to draw a simple picture of each beatitude in the squares. Allow time for each person to explain his or her drawings.

—NANCY STALLARD

29
Wisdom from Water: Fulfillment

In the small group we lead at Southwest Missouri State, many of the women were struggling with their to-do lists. Even when they managed to accomplish everything, they still felt empty. So in our Bible study one night, we addressed fulfillment.

We labeled a dozen clear, plastic cups according to the things that filled our lives, such as school, jobs, appearance, worry, and friends. (We did not leave a cup for time with God.) Then we gave each person a cup full of water with her name on it and explained that the water represented her time and energy. Everyone was to pour the amount of water into the labeled cups proportionate to the amount of time she spent on that activity.

After everyone finished, we talked about which cups were the fullest. The "worry" cup, for example, was nearly overflowing. Then we looked at how much water, if any, we had left in the cups with our names on them. We pointed out that we often give only the water remaining—which is very little—to God. This is why we feel empty even after accomplishing our to-do lists.

We discussed ways we could pour water back into our cups, such as giving our burdens to the Lord so we didn't worry as much, or accepting fewer hours at work. Finally, we talked about how God wants to fill us to overflowing. We brainstormed ways to allow Him to do this, such as quiet time, Bible study, prayer, and using our gifts. This was a powerful and effective lesson for all of us.

—NICHOLE QUIGLEY AND CRYSTEN COY

30
You've Got Mail:
The Attributes of God

Our small group was ending its study on the attributes of God. Earlier in the study, I had asked the group members to keep good notes, because they would need them later for a project.

On the last day, I gave each person an envelope and a piece of paper, and asked them to spend a few minutes answering the following questions: Which attribute of God has blessed you most? Why did it stand out?

After they had finished, I instructed them to seal the notes in the envelopes and address the envelope to themselves. I collected the envelopes and told them that I would mail them after praying over when to send the notes.

One by one, I sent the letters. Many group members shared how they experienced God's perfect timing; often, notes came as people were facing personal challenges, and the letters reminded them of specific attributes of God that could meet their immediate circumstances.

—ANNETTE KELLY

31
It's a Wrap: Review and Application

Our group meets weekly for Bible study. We set aside the last meeting of the month as Reexamination Night. We begin by reviewing what we've learned that month. We reread the relevant verses from each study and summarize the lessons. Next, we discuss questions and concerns from the month's material. Then we answer the questions, How has this lesson become real in our lives? and, How can we make this lesson more real in our lives?

We close by praising God for growth we've seen and praying for areas in which we still need to apply His truth. Reexamination Night ensures we won't forget what we've learned and will be faithful to apply Scripture to our lives. It is also an excellent opportunity for those who missed a week of study to catch up.

—Angela Dion

Prayer

Enriching Group Prayer

32
Introducing a New Believer to Group Prayer

When new Christians join your small group, they may be unacquainted with the how-to's of prayer, and thus reluctant to pray aloud. This will be especially true if they've come to associate public praying with flowery language. Here are some ideas for making prayer less threatening.

- *Indirect praying.* Allow members of the group to express what they're thankful for. Then one person who feels comfortable doing so can read or recite the list in prayer on behalf of the whole group.
- *Open eyes.* Pray with your eyes open. This may seem odd to the veterans in the group, but it can take some of the mystery out of the prayer experience and reinforce the truth that prayer is conversation.
- *Pray conversationally.* Remind the group of how an ordinary conversation progresses—with a topic being mentioned, others commenting on the topic, that topic leading to a related one, and so on. Then talk to God in the same way. Designate someone to begin with praise, with anyone contributing aloud who wishes to do so. Praise will generally lead to thanksgiving, again with people randomly voicing their thanks aloud (no praying around the circle!). Thanksgiving flows into reminders of ongoing needs and personal requests. After a certain time, the small-group leader can close the prayer "conversation."
- *Open-ended praying.* You may feel led, during the prayer time, to read Scripture to the group, or to ask questions of someone about a personal need, and then return to talking to God. As the group experiences intimacy with each other and with God, this free flow of conversation (both vertically and horizontally) will become easier.

—JANICE HARRIS

33
Praying the Night Away

If you're looking for a great way to spend an evening with your small group, try a half-night of prayer. This works best on a weekend evening, when it's most convenient for people to gather from 6 p.m. till midnight. The extended time allows your group to get into a deep spirit of prayer. Plan a variety of activities to keep the evening interesting. Here are some ideas to stimulate your creativity.

- *Praise.* To set the right tone for the evening—one of gratitude and expectation—begin by giving praise and thanks to God.
- *Scripture prayers.* Say prayers aloud that incorporate favorite Bible passages. Or select several prayers from Scripture. Read them together, or have everyone reflect silently as someone else reads aloud.
- *Sanctuary prayer blitz.* Go into the church sanctuary. Move throughout the room, asking the Lord to bless people through what happens there. For example, stand in the pulpit and pray for your pastor and his sermons. Among the pews, pray for church members. Stand at the door and pray for greeters and visitors.
- *Silent confession.* Allow people to go off alone to confess their sins to God. (You may want to provide some brief teaching on confession and guidelines for how to do this.) When you reconvene, be sure to communicate unconditional forgiveness through Christ.
- *Drive-by prayers.* Pile into cars and drive around town. Pray for schools, nursing homes, Christian ministries, and churches you pass. (It's okay for the driver to keep his eyes open!)
- *Jericho march around city hall.* Pray for government officials, pending legislation, and that Jesus' will would be done in your city.
- *God's view.* Go to the top of your town's tallest building and pray over your city. Pray for what you see in each direction.
- *Reflection and sharing.* Allow 20–30 minutes for people to share what they learned and how they experienced God. Order pizza or sip hot chocolate at midnight to celebrate a meaningful evening in prayer.

—KEITH D. WRIGHT

34
Prayer Concerts

In many nonWestern churches, Christians often pray aloud—all at the same time. The idea is simply to lift individual prayers to God in concert. Try it with your small group. Perhaps you will want to share requests first. Then all participants will pray at once in low voices. No one hears specific words, just murmurs. The sound this makes is beautifully soothing. Imagine what it sounds like to God!

This form of prayer helps people keep their focus on God and prevents their minds from wandering while someone else is talking to the Lord.

—Michael Mack

35
Practicing Prayer

One evening, our small group talked about why prayer was often the first thing dropped when our days got busy. We listed several obstacles that seemed to keep us from the prayer life we all desired. We then ended the night by practicing several approaches to prayer.

I had set up six prayer stations around the room and posted an index card at each one with clear instructions. I described the stations to the group and explained that we would all start at separate stations and rotate every five minutes so that we could experience a variety of ways of praying. I kept an eye on the clock and moved to the next station when it was time to rotate. Each person took a paper and pen along, because several stations involved writing. Here are the six stations we used.

Station One—Pray following the ACTS pattern. Start with Adoration, then move on to Confession and Thanksgiving; end with Supplication.

Station Two—Pray prayers that others have prayed. (I marked some in a Bible and copied some from *Discipleship Journal* (see "Borrowed Prayers," by Timothy Jones, Issue 125 at http://www.navpress.com/magazines/DJ/Article Display/125.09).

Station Three—Write a prayer to God.

Station Four—Create a list of what you're thankful for, and thank God for His blessings.

Station Five—Be still and listen to God, fighting all distractions. Write down what you're hearing.

Station Six—Pray through worship. Rejoice in the Lord by jumping up and down, sitting still, kneeling, walking around, and so on. I provided a boom box with a worship CD—and headphones—for group members to listen to.

We left the meeting refreshed. We had touched the heart of God and had confidence we could do it again throughout the week.

—Nichole Quigley

36
Seven Ways to Enrich Group Prayer

Variety is the spice of life—and of small-group prayer times. Get away from the weekly grind of sharing requests, praying for requests, and immediately forgetting requests with these ideas.

- *Teach about prayer.* Point group members to the practical insights given in Scripture. Look together at prayers that are recorded in the Bible. They can teach you how to praise, give thanks, make requests, confess, and so on.
- *Pray directly to God.* Instead of sharing prayer requests with one another and then repeating them to God, ask people to give their requests directly to God. For example, someone might say, "Lord, I have a situation at work that's becoming stressful." Group members can then join in with sentence prayers for wisdom, patience, a sense of God's presence, and so forth.
- *Encourage unity in prayer* by "directing" silent prayer time for each request. You might say, "Lord, we pray for Jill as she prepares for her upcoming exam." Then let a minute pass while people pray in silent unity for Jill. Continue with the other requests in the same manner.
- *Finish a sentence.* For example: "One of the best things about you, God, is . . ." or, "I love you, Lord, because . . ." or, "Lord, I'm wondering . . ."
- *Encourage prayer journaling* and share from your own journal on occasion.

- *Gather written prayers from various sources.* Assign one prayer to an individual to pray during the week and then bring it back to read during group prayer time. This works especially well if you can gather prayers written about a specific theme you're studying.
- *Learn to relax with silence.* The psalmist wrote, "Be still, and know that I am God" (Psalm 46:10). Remind group members that it's not what we say that brings us into prayer. It's God Himself who draws us to His heart. Learn to rest in His presence.

—MARSHA CROCKETT

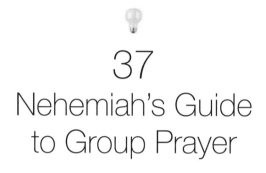

37
Nehemiah's Guide to Group Prayer

Has the prayer time in your small group become a routine recital of wish lists by each member? Breaking out of this rut is a challenge for any group leader. The trick is to turn the focus from your desires to God's. A brief look at Nehemiah 1:5-11 shows four steps that can help your group focus its prayers.

- *Focus on who God is and what He has done for you* (verses 5-6). When Nehemiah heard that the walls of Jerusalem were destroyed, his prayers focused on who God is, not on the problems at hand. He called God awesome, the One who keeps His covenant of love. He reminded God that He listens to His servants' prayers. Your group can begin by praising God for His wonderful creation, His gift of salvation, His love and mercy. Thank God for answered prayer and for specific blessings.
- *Focus on who you are before God* (verses 6-7). Nehemiah confesses for himself, his household, and for the entire nation of Israel. He says in verse 7, "We have acted very wickedly toward you. We have not obeyed the commands, decrees and laws you gave your servant Moses." Sometimes we forget who God is and who is serving whom. We need to remember that we are His servants and that we have failed Him at times. As a group we can corporately confess for our families, our country, and ourselves.
- *Focus on what God says in His Word* (verses 8-9). In the same way Nehemiah quoted God's own words to Him, a portion of Scripture will

often help focus your prayers. Ask group members to read passages that ministered to them during the week, or have verses ready that everyone can read together.

- *Focus on your petitions* (verses 10-11). God wants us to ask Him to meet our needs. Nehemiah doesn't give God a list or tell Him how to answer. Preparing to go before the king, he merely asks God to "Give [His] servant success today by granting him favor in the presence of this man" (verse 11).

After we focus on who God is, who we are before Him, and what His Word says, our prayer requests take on a new perspective. We pray more for the spiritual needs of our loved ones and ourselves, seeking God's heart in all things.

—Patricia Perry

38
Prayer with a Focus

When our Bible study group committed to a special prayer focus for the year—the salvation of nonChristian family and friends—we experienced the joy of welcoming several new brothers and sisters into Christ's family.

Consider enhancing the normal exchange of prayer requests in your small group by committing to a prayer focus for at least one quarter. Choose any issue the Lord impresses on your group members. Ideas include

- *Missions.* List the missionaries your church supports, and pray for each one individually, including their families. Stay updated on physical, financial, or spiritual needs. Lift up the community they are reaching for Christ. Ask God to give strength to those facing persecution for spreading the gospel.
- *Your pastors and their families.* Pray for their children and spouses, wisdom in their ministry, and protection against temptation and spiritual attack.
- *New ministries.* As your church starts new outreaches or programs, make these your group's prayer priority. Pray that people will find Christ and that programs will meet needs.
- *Children and teens of the congregation.* List the children of your group members, of your church staff, kids with special needs, or all the children at church. Pray for specific situations as well as their salvation,

protection in school, encouragement as they grow, and boldness in sharing their faith.

- *Your individual neighborhoods.* We are all surrounded by neighbors who don't know the Lord, or who live in difficult circumstances, or who are simply new to the community. Pray for the neighborhoods of each of your members. Ask God for opportunities to witness and invite neighbors to church. Pray that each of you will be an example for Christ in the way you speak, react to conflicts, and respond to needs.

—JEANETTE HANSCOME

39
Enlarging Your World

To keep your small group focused on the Great Commission, choose a country each week to pray for. Make use of your local newspaper, "Church Around the World" updates (often available through your local church), or *Operation World* by Patrick Johnstone. During your intercessory prayer time, make it a habit to pray not just for each other but also for your "country-of-the-week."

—DENISE BOUCHARD

Prayer

Praying for Each Other

40
In the Spotlight

Our small group assigned one person each week to be the spotlight of our prayers. The "spotlight" shares her praises and requests in as much or as little detail as she chooses. Then we usually break into groups of three or four to pray for her.

When we first began this practice, some people were timid about sharing. But the blessings of being prayed for have outweighed the brief discomfort at being the center of attention. The group's level of intimacy has deepened, and we have encouraged one another with stories of answered prayer.

—CARRIE SCHULIGER

41
Photo Reminders

Our Bible study leader took individual photographs of our small group members. Each week we exchange pictures and pray for the person we picked. Having pictures of one another helps us to personalize prayer requests and reminds us to pray.

—KATHY TSUCHIYAMA

42
Pass the Mug, Please

Our leader made each of us a coffee mug at a pottery store. One side bore our names. On the other side was a personalized prayer of Jabez (see 1 Chronicles

4:10), for example, "Oh, that you would bless Sue and enlarge her territory! Let your hand be with Sue, and keep her from harm."

Each week we fill our mugs with candy, hot chocolate packets, or other treats and bring them to our meeting. There, we exchange mugs. In the days that follow, whenever we drink from the new mug, we pray for the person it belongs to. And we know someone else is sipping coffee and whispering our names in prayer, too.

—Sue Skalicky

43
You Paged?

At our small-group meetings, we always pray for members going through difficulties. But for those who are suffering, the days between group meetings can be long and lonely. That's why we added a new dimension to our prayer coverage—a prayer pager. We give the hurting group member a pager, and the rest of us write down the pager number. Each time a call is placed, the pager vibrates and displays a message saying, "I am praying for you." Those who have carried the pager during times of crisis have experienced an outpouring of love and support through hundreds of pages.

—Sue Skalicky

Worship

44
On the Record

Purchase a small, inexpensive spiral notebook for each group member in which to record prayer requests each time your group meets. On a regular basis, perhaps quarterly, replace your regular small-group format with an evening of praise in which you go back through your prayer journals and give God thanks and praise for His answers. If your group enjoys singing, incorporate some praise choruses into this special evening. Make it a celebration of God's faithfulness.

—SUE KLINE

45
Praising God's Names

Though He is the same yesterday, today, and forever, God's name changes as He reveals Himself to His people in the midst of their circumstances. For instance, He revealed Himself as "our deliverer" when my wife and I encountered a hostile man while witnessing. We know who He is because of His actions.

Here is an exercise to help your small-group members see with new eyes how God is working in their lives. Start by providing each person with a list of God's names that you find in Scripture. For example:

- God who saves me (see Psalm 51:14)
- My confidence (see Psalm 71:5)
- A consuming fire (see Deuteronomy 4:24)
- My friend (see Job 16:20)
- Wonderful Counselor (see Isaiah 9:6)
- God of all comfort (see 2 Corinthians 1:3)
- God who avenges me (see Psalm 18:47)

For a more complete list, refer to a topical study Bible or to resources such as the *Experiencing God* Bible study workbook by Henry Blackaby and Claude King.

Now ask each person to complete the following sentence: Because of what He has done for me, today God's name is _____. Take turns explaining why God has become that name to you recently. Then devote some time to praising God for what you've learned about His character through His names.

—CLARK COTHERN

46
Worshiping with the Word

Many churches use worship choruses as part of their services. But some people may not know that some of the lyrics come directly from Scripture. If your small group enjoys music, examine favorite songs by digging into the Bible. You could investigate one song a week or do an entire lesson that covers several.

You can use a couple of different approaches: Start with the song; use a concordance to look up key words to discover if the song is based on a particular passage. Or start with the passage, and have your group identify the song contained within.

Either way, read surrounding verses to understand the context. Then discuss how the verses add depth to the chorus. Be sure to sing the song together. You'll find that knowing the scriptural basis of your worship songs enhances both your worship and your Bible reading.

To get you started, here are some songs and their scriptural counterparts. The worship leader at your church may also be able to direct you to specific choruses used in your services.

- Psalm 18:3   I Will Call upon the Lord
- Psalm 47:1   Clap Your Hands
- Psalm 51:10-12   Create in Me a Clean Heart
- Psalm 57:5,11   Be Exalted
- Psalm 73:25-26   God Is the Strength of My Life
- Psalm 84:10   Better Is One Day
- Psalm 95:6-7   Come Let Us Worship and Bow Down
- Psalm 97:1-6   The Lord Reigns
- Psalm 97:9   We Exalt Thee
- Psalm 118:24   This Is the Day
- Proverbs 18:10   The Name of the Lord
- Revelation 5:13   To Him Who Sits on the Throne

—CAROL R. COOL

47
Cures for Wilting Worship

What does it take to use music effectively in a small group? Here are some of the ideas sent by *DJ* readers who enjoy their small-group singing.

- As the group arrives, have an instrumental worship tape playing softly. This will set a worshipful tone. Or, if the group has a guitarist, ask him to play softly as people arrive. It's then easy to move into singing.
- Select songs that everyone knows. Having to follow unfamiliar words on a song sheet can be distracting. However, if your small group has newcomers in it each week, song sheets will make them feel more comfortable.
- Once or twice a year, devote an entire small-group meeting to worship. Ask someone from your church's worship team to join you and lead the worship.
- Here's another activity for a worship evening. Ask group members to come prepared to relate their favorite hymn or praise song and tell why it is meaningful to them.
- Select songs that focus on one theme. It may be one of God's attributes, such as His faithfulness. Or perhaps your songs will reflect your Bible study topic.
- Sing to tapes. The voices on the tape may give your group members more confidence to join in. After all, for the shy or the tone-deaf, singing in a small group is much more intimidating than singing in a large congregation.
- The most upbeat songs work best with larger groups (ten or more). The more mellow worship songs work well in a group of any size.

Small-group singing may not sound as impressive as congregational singing, but small groups bring intimacy to the worship experience. The best small groups create an atmosphere of acceptance that encourages spontaneity and transparency.

48
Worship for the Musically Challenged

You know worship is an important element of small-group life. But you tried group singing a few tunes and it was a disaster. Your entire group is tone deaf! Take heart. There are ways to build worship into your meetings without torturing the nonmusical.

- *Psalms.* The psalms are beautiful when sung. But they are also beautiful when read aloud. And their down-to-earth language engages our emotions and gives us words to express our worship. There are several ways to read the psalms for group worship. Use a psalm as a responsive reading, in which the leader reads the first verse then the group reads the next verse, and so on. Or read a psalm a few verses at a time, pausing between passages to allow time for group members to meditate on the words. Some psalms—especially the praise ones—are wonderful to read in unison.
- *Silence.* Perhaps your group doesn't like to sing. But you can still incorporate music. Ask group members to quietly reflect and pray while you play a taped instrumental version of a few familiar worship songs or a stirring classical piece such as Bach's *Jesu Joy of Man's Desiring* or Rachmaninoff's *Vespers* or Handel's *Messiah*. Or prepare hearts for Bible study by finding a recorded song with lyrics that touch on the message of that night's lesson. This is an excellent way to refocus after a stressful day of work, parenting, and so on.
- *Readings.* Select a devotional reading or Scripture passage to read aloud. Look for material that will help you focus on God in worship and wonder. *Knowing God* by J. I. Packer, *The Knowledge of the Holy* by A. W. Tozer, and *My Utmost for His Highest* by Oswald Chambers are my personal favorites.
- *The Book of Common Prayer.* This traditional worship book is full of material to help your group express thanksgiving, praise, confession, and so forth.
- *Hymnals.* You don't have to sing hymns, you know. You can read them.

Does someone in your group have an expressive reading style? Ask him or her to read the lyrics of a hymn aloud, then have everyone offer sentence prayers of praise for what the hymn teaches about the ways of God.

—Sue Kline

49
Kick Off with Praise

"It is good to praise the Lord" (Psalm 92:1). Our small group has adopted this verse as an opening to our meetings. As we offer our praises to God, it helps us focus our thoughts on His many attributes, such as His kindness and compassion toward us.

Some members read an entire psalm. Others read selected verses. One woman wrote a beautiful prayer of praise and thanksgiving that she read for our group. Our times of praise enhance the intercession that follows and set a wonderful tone for the remainder of our meeting.

—Betty Thompson

Fellowship

Getting to Know You: Exercises to Help Group
Members Learn About Each Other

50
What's in a Name?

Distribute sheets of paper (or blank name tags) and tell group members to write their first name vertically on the left side of the paper. Then ask them to make an acrostic from their name that tells something about their personality, employment, hobbies, past experiences, and so on. For example, P could stand for "promotion." R could refer to a recent "relocation." L could represent "loss" and refer to anything from a weight loss to the death of a loved one. Y could stand for "yogurt," a favorite food.

Now, give each person time to explain his or her acrostic to the rest of the group. This can also work in a large group if you divide into huddles of four to six people for the sharing time.

—Terry Powell

51
Grab Bags

For an icebreaker in a new group, ask each person to bring a bag with three small items in it. These items should tell us something about the person's life. In our group, one man brought a computer disk, a golf ball, and a slice of bread. The computer disk reflected his occupation, the golf ball his favorite sport, and the bread his baking hobby. Another man said, "I bake bread, too!" They began to exchange recipes and ideas for sharing their bread.

There are a number of variations on this activity. For example, you could ask members to bring three items that reveal something about where they grew up, then try guessing the locales.

—Joan Fredrickson

52
Candyland

Once group members are settled, pass a large bag of M&M's and invite everyone to take a handful, but not to eat them yet. Next, explain that each color corresponds with a personal disclosure by group members. For example, every brown candy is a fact about where they grew up. Every red candy is a story about work. Green candies call for a story of faith, blue an embarrassing moment, and so on. You can adapt your categories to fit your group.

As people tell about themselves, the group begins to form a set of shared stories and experiences. It also acquires its own set of hilarious moments, mostly coming from group members who take huge handfuls of candy and have to share 20 embarrassing moments! Charitable group leaders will let that person off the hook in the interest of ending the meeting before midnight!

—Michael Mumme

53
On the Hot Seat

Our group has learned more about each other through the hot seat. Each week a different group member volunteers to be on the hot seat for 15–20 minutes. During this time, other members can ask anything they want. The only rule is that the person on the hot seat can refuse to answer any question. (So far, no one has ever refused.) Through this exercise we learn things about each other that might never have come out otherwise.

—John Goodale

54
Where in the World?

When our new small group began, I brought an old map of the world and laid it out in the center of the room. I then gave each person a different-colored felt marker, and one by one we marked the geographical pathways of our lives.

Beginning with where we were born, we each traced our journey to the present. Conversation emerged naturally as we plotted and described where we had lived. People were surprised and delighted to find that paths had unknowingly crossed in the past. Questions came easily as group members asked why someone moved so often, or wondered about the feelings certain moves invoked.

We then plotted on the map where our grandparents came from. We found some had emigrated from other countries. This launched a discussion about origins and experiences growing up in a recent-immigrant family. All in all, tracing our journeys provided interesting information that would otherwise have been difficult to volunteer.

Our prayers that evening focused on thanking God for the richness and diversity of our pasts and our desire to learn from and with each other in the group.

—Bob Rose

55
Just the Facts

A few days in advance of your small-group meeting, call members and ask for three little-known facts about them. Type these facts in random order, leaving a wide margin to the left of each fact. At your next meeting, give a fact sheet plus a pencil to each group member. Explain that they are to place to the left of each fact the name of the person they believe fits the fact. Set a time limit of five or ten minutes. Provide a humorous prize for the person who matches the most facts with the correct people.

This is a great way to learn new things about each other, whether your group has been together for years or for weeks.

—Rose Yoder

Fellowship

Building Deeper Relationships

56
Jiffy Small-Group Retreats

"Connectedness" is what many people desire in a small group. Yet the weekly group meeting is often focused more on study than socializing. Quarterly informal retreats can effectively meet relational needs without being expensive or extensive. Here are four types of retreats that meet different small-group needs.

The Shared Experience Retreat
When friendships are new, hold your getaway nearby.
- Rent a retreat center or lodge for one night and split the cost. Take in a movie, concert, or museum, and use the rest of the evening for conversation. Sleep late the next morning and be home by noon.
- Relocate one family and invade their home. Plan a gourmet dinner menu and create it together. Encourage each person to bring something to share after dinner: a favorite book to review, a craft to teach, a question to debate, and so on.

The Ministry Retreat
As friendships gel, plan retreats with a purpose.
- Select one group member's house for an overnight retreat (relocate the rest of the family). Choose a long-neglected house project that the hostess needs done—washing windows, sorting photos, putting in a garden. Work a full day and then go out for dinner.
- Try the same setup, but select someone outside the group (perhaps a single mom or a widow) for the day's work project.

The Planning Retreat
- Discuss your current topic of study. Is it helping? How could the study be improved? What applications have been made as a result of the study?
- Evaluate books for future study topics.
- Record physical, spiritual, family, and personal goals.

The Prayer Retreat
Go someplace where you can get lost in nature.

- Plan time to be alone with God to read Scripture and pray.
- Allow unscheduled time to listen to God speak.
- Reconvene for prayer and praise.

—SANDY CLARK

57
This Is Your Life

Nothing has given our small group a greater sense of community in a short amount of time than sharing our life stories. We give each member an entire evening to tell his or her story. Some people enhance their stories with pictures, props, or videos. Life stories can be historical, moving from childhood through the present, including salvation testimonies and other significant events. Or they can focus on more current events and tell what God has taught or done recently in a person's life.

Remind people that this is not a business presentation—polish isn't important. Many will find it useful, however, to have an outline or some bulleted points to help them keep their train of thought. Encourage people to be transparent. Include significant struggles as well as funny anecdotes. Above all, make your life story a testimony to God's goodness. The leader should set the tone by going first.

In our group, the presenter began his or her story immediately after our icebreaker. I'd suggest allowing 30 minutes for this. That will leave time for people to ask questions throughout the story and interact with the presenter. It will also leave time for your group to pray for the member whose story you just heard. I encourage group members to take notes—these often help identify areas of common interest and enable more informed prayer.

We spent a summer sharing our life stories. You may want to do one life story a month as a break from your normal routine. Or ask group members to share their life stories as their birthdays come around.

Throughout this activity, our group laughed a lot and grew in our empathy for and closeness to one another. Even now, nearly two years later, we are a more united group because we shared our stories.

—DAVID B. REID

58
If I Were a Board Game

Sometimes a silly icebreaker can promote deep discussion in your small-group meeting. Although lighthearted, the following questions prompt a surprising level of self-evaluation. Perhaps they will do so for your small group—and provide a few laughs along the way.

- If your life right now was a game, which of the following would it be and why?

The Dating Game	Clue
Aggravation	Sorry!
Hungry Hippos	Scruples
Payday	Boggle
The Game of Life	Mouse Trap
Candy Land	Taboo
Battleship	Concentration
Scrabble	Let's Go Fishin'
Twister	Solitaire
Trivial Pursuit	Risk
Trouble	

- Which magazine title best describes the present state of your relationship with God? How or why?

Air and Space	*Hope*
Breakaway	*Insight*
Child Life	*Marriage Partnership*
Christian History	*Modern Bride*
Cruise	*Moody*
Discover	*New Man*
Games	*New Woman*
Good Housekeeping	*Outdoor Life*
Grit	*Pray!*
Guideposts	*Runners World*
Healthy Living	

- If the current state of your relationships was given a television show or movie title, which of the following would it be? Why?

Home Alone	*The Big Chill*
The Sound of Music	*That's Entertainment!*
It's a Wonderful Life	*The Hiding Place*
Field of Dreams	*The Fugitive*
Time Chasers	*Great Expectations*
The Neverending Story	*Gone with the Wind*
The Outsiders	*The Odd Couple*
Spin City	*Nowhere to Run*
E.R.	*Independence Day*
Sports Night	*Cape Fear*
Dirty Rotten Scoundrels	*Disclosure*

59
Every Picture Tells a Story

Recently in my Bible study group, I passed around a picture from the cover of a book on marriage. I was amazed at my group members' responses when I asked them, "What emotions do you feel when you look at this picture?" Answers included:

"I don't believe that picture. I wish it was true, but no couple has intimacy like that."

"I think of warm emotions, feeling loved, cared about."

"Wow! That's me and my husband!"

"Too intimate for me."

"Looks like a troubled marriage. Maybe they're making up after a fight."

Wow! I thought. I've learned more about these people with one picture and one question than I normally learn in several meetings!

To duplicate this exercise, search for an intriguing picture that allows for interpretation by the viewer. Ask group members to pass around the picture, allowing each person time to determine what emotions the picture evokes.

Hand out slips of paper on which members can jot down their responses to the picture. (This prevents people from changing their answers after hearing the comments of others.)

The amazingly different ways we experience a picture reveal a chunk of our own hidden hearts.

—BOBBIE YAGEL

60
Job Sharing

In order to better support each other, our group developed the "Work-world Project." This project gave us insight into group members' job-related stresses, ministry opportunities, and prayer needs.

Our group began by filling out a questionnaire at home. Then we brought our sheets to the next meeting and shared answers. Eventually the answers were collected, typed up, and made into small booklets for each group member.

As we gained more insight into friends' jobs, we began to pray more specifically. When we came into contact with others who did similar jobs, we found that the lessons we learned from this project provided common ground to open conversations.

Our undertaking also provided resource people we could introduce to new acquaintances. For example, when an orthodontist moved into a friend's subdivision, a guy who's in our small group chatted with him and then said, "I know a great guy in my prayer group who's a dentist. I bet you'd enjoy meeting him."

If your group would like to try this project, start by filling out a questionnaire similar to ours.

- How did you get into your profession?
- What's the hardest thing about your job?
- What's the most enjoyable or satisfying part of your profession?
- How can others pray for you regarding your work life?
- What is your typical workday like?
- How do you serve Christ through your job?
- In what specific ways can we support you in your job?
- If you were trying to lead a nonbeliever to Christ and the only ground you had in common with that person was your profession, what job-related analogy could you use to explain the gospel? (This question is best assigned as long-term "homework." It will require more thought than most of the other questions.)

Through this project our group members came to understand each other better, to appreciate and face our jobs with new enthusiasm, and to remember that the Lord places us in the work world so we can participate in His work every day.

—Rhonda Reese

61
Discovery Dates

One of the secrets to a strong marriage is to continue dating. Our couples' group chose to apply this principle to our group relationships as well. Once a month we went on a group date.

Because the typical date is a passive dinner and movie, we declared such dates off-limits. Instead, we sought dates that were either active or interactive. We tried dance lessons, pottery painting, laser tag, scuba lessons, miniature golf, billiards, and board games.

These dates provided great nights of laughter and enjoying one another's company. They not only helped to spice up group life, but they also helped put some fun back into our marriages.

—Brian Mavis

62
Discover Your Inner Child

Throw a Second-Childhood Party for your small group. Forget "adult" activities such as bridge, cribbage, or Trivial Pursuit. Instead, set up play stations throughout your house with cans of Play-Doh, zillions of pipe cleaners, coloring books and crayons, jacks, marbles, construction paper and paste, and building blocks. Serve truly sophisticated party fare—colored popcorn, cupcakes, Kool-Aid, peanut-butter-and-jelly finger sandwiches, dinosaur-shaped Jell-O chunks, and so on. The purpose? Pure fun and a way to unwind from the demands of adult life.

—Sue Kline

63
Three Cheers for Traditions

Families have traditions. Some return to the same vacation spot every year. Others stick to the same menu for Christmas dinner, decade after decade, and woe to anyone who suggests a variation! Others follow certain rituals for planting a garden each spring or celebrating a child's birthday. Traditions underline the seasons of life while at the same time lending a sense of continuity. They give us a sense of security.

Small groups at their best are a form of family. If your small group is still struggling to find that family spirit, perhaps you need some traditions. One group attends a Shakespeare-in-the-Park performance every summer. Another goes trout fishing annually. Some groups have traditions to mark holidays—serving up turkey and fixings at a community Thanksgiving dinner for the homeless, caroling at retirement homes, decorating their church's sanctuary with lilies for Easter. Then there are the men's nights out at the ball park, or the women's pajama parties. And berry picking in the spring or apple picking in the fall. Traditions don't require a lot of money or extensive planning—just a joy in being together.

Look back on some of the activities your group has tried together. Which have brought the most enjoyment? Plan to repeat them next year—you could have a tradition in the making. Or if you're a newly formed group, order in some pizza one evening and brainstorm activities you'd like to try together.

—SUE KLINE

64
Family Meals

Our small group meets midweek and most of us work outside the home. By the time we get home, change clothes, eat dinner, and rush to our small-group meeting, we're frazzled and distracted.

That's why we decided to eat together. We plan meals with lots of ingredients (salad bar, burrito night, pasta bar, build-your-own sandwiches, and so on) to which we all contribute. Because many of us didn't eat together as families growing up, our small-group "family" meals have been great for everyone involved. Eating together allows us to unwind, catch up on news, and be ready to focus on Bible study an hour later. It has also helped us get to know one another better, which gives us more freedom to share honestly during our study.

—Joanne Heim

65
Listening Makes Cents

Are your small-group members good listeners? Here's one way to find out.

Give each person in your group five pennies. Then divide into groups of three and provide the groups with a current news story or a Bible passage to discuss. Explain the ground rules: "When you speak, you must spend one penny. No one else may interrupt while you are speaking. When you have finished your comment, you must let someone else spend a penny and speak."

Once everyone has spent the pennies, come together as one group again and discuss the following questions.

- Did you find it easy or hard to follow the rules of this exercise? Why?
- Did any of you run out of pennies before you ran out of things to say? Did any of you find it hard to spend all your pennies?
- What comments did other group members make that let you know they were listening? What body language did they use to say, "I'm hearing you"?
- Did you find you had more thoughts on the subject than you expected? Did you feel your contributions to the group were appreciated? What made you feel that way?
- Did the awareness of listening more carefully make the conversation more effective or less effective? Could this exercise improve our Bible study discussion? How?
- What would happen if Christians practiced better listening before responding to nonChristians? What would listening do for other relationships—with workmates, friends, relatives, your spouse?

—Clark Cothern

66
Divided We Stand

In an effort to deepen relationships with one another and work through common struggles, the men in our couples' small group decided to get together separately. These meetings are in addition to our twice-a-month coed gatherings. We explore how to apply the Bible to issues we face at home and work. We also try to create an environment of healthy accountability in our walk with Christ.

This idea was so well received that the women in our group decided to follow suit. Now both men and women meet twice a month in gender-specific groups. On alternate weeks, we meet as a coed group. We've all been blessed by this additional opportunity to deepen relationships.

—Jon Hilgenkamp

67
When I Was Twenty-Five

For our twenty-fifth meeting, I asked our small-group members to bring a personal photo from when they were age twenty-five and to come prepared to share some personal events from that year. Our evening was a big hit!

One couple had to go back more than sixty years in their memory banks. For our members under thirty-five, this proved very enlightening. Sharing such diverse experiences and hearing how God had worked in our lives brought us closer together.

—Betty Thompson

68
Celebrating Each Other

When our group came to the end of a study, we decided to celebrate each other during our final potluck. In our discussion, we named each person and said, "I see Jesus the _____ in you." The blank was filled with Jesus the Servant, the Prophet, the Teacher, the Healer, the Miracle Worker, the Shepherd, and so on.

Starting with one person, everyone shared what it was about her that reminded us of Jesus and why. We learned how the other group members valued us. We also learned how Jesus was using us to show Himself to others in a way we would have never known otherwise. After we each celebrated one person, we asked for her prayer request and then prayed over her by laying on hands.

—Henriet Schapelhouman

69
Gone but Not Forgotten

While you're basking in the fellowship and enjoying the spiritual (and sometimes physical) food provided by a small group, it's hard to imagine that you might someday disband. But schedules shift, leaders relocate, family situations change. Any number of factors may make it impossible for your group to continue meeting. Fellowship can continue, however, on a less formal basis. My husband and I belonged to two small groups that disbanded, but we have stayed in touch in other ways.

- *A birthday club.* We get together when any member has a birthday. Usually we eat at a restaurant and exchange humorous cards. Sometimes we meet at a home for pizza and games. Once, a couple hosted a murder mystery dinner, using a kit purchased at a game store.
- *Reuniting to care.* One of our members now lives in a personal care home. A few times a year, the rest of us visit her. We share a meal or snack with her, have devotions, sing, and pray together. She is always delighted to see us, and the rest of us receive a huge blessing as well.

- *Shared activities.* Other groups might choose to stay in touch through an occasional hike followed by a stop at an ice cream store, taking on a group mission project such as helping to serve at a local soup kitchen, or helping each other with home or landscape projects. Any activity you've enjoyed as a small group can become a continued source of fellowship after your formal meetings have ended.

We discovered that the ties we formed as we studied God's Word together did not have to be broken when our situations changed. With flexibility, creativity, and commitment we've been able to forge timeless relationships with these friends.

—Kelly Allred

Outreach

Missions

70
Ideas for Global-Minded Groups

To get people involved in the church around the world, we must stir them to think about global realities, cross-cultural relationships, and a world much bigger than our own. Here are a few ideas for stimulating interest in other cultures.

- Identify and pray for friends, neighbors, and coworkers who are internationals.
- Identify and pray for friends, neighbors, and coworkers who adhere to other world religions: Hinduism, Islam, Buddhism, and so on.
- Get an up-to-date map, choose a country per meeting, and pray for Christians living in those countries. *Operation World* by Patrick Johnstone is a good resource for prayer information.
- Take a group field trip to a local mosque, Hindu temple, or synagogue, and try to interview the religious leader. Don't make this an evangelistic effort, but simply learn about the beliefs of others.
- Go to an ethnic restaurant and seek out the owners or hosts with the goal of interviewing them about their culture, religious beliefs, and—if they are immigrants—their experiences in your country.
- Assign group members specific countries or nationalities to research on the Internet, asking the members to bring a one-page summary to the rest of the group.
- Go together to a Christian worship service that is different from yours either culturally or ethnically. Use this opportunity to remind yourselves that God's people constitute a broad range of races and ethnicities. Reflect on Revelation 7:9 as you worship, and remind yourselves that you are part of God's global village.

—Paul Borthwick

71
What in the World
Is Going On?

One way to expose your group members to what God is doing around the world is to have each person subscribe to a mission agency's publication (or perhaps you can obtain copies from your church library). Each person can pick an area of the world he or she is interested in.

Ask group members to choose one article from their magazine to share with the group. You can do this on an alternating basis—a different person each time you meet. Your group will grow more mindful of the world's needs and of the great things God is doing among myriad peoples.

—BRADLEY AUCOIN

72
Encouraging Teen Missionaries

More and more teens are using their summer breaks for mission travel. For some, these trips open the door to mission work for life. Others return to their daily lives as more committed believers who infect their peers with a deeper faith.

Your small group can become an integral part of a teen missionary's support team. Here's how:
- *Identify your partner.* Ask your pastor for a list of teens from your church who are preparing for a summer mission. Pray over the list as a group, and identify which teen you will "adopt."
- *Provide encouragement.* Notes of encouragement can go a long way in keeping your teen's spirits high, especially during the difficult task of fund-raising.
- *Provide financial support.* Consider making a group donation to the teen's fund-raising efforts. Participate in events such as car washes or bake sales.

- *Keep in touch.* Send e-mails and letters while your teen is away. Plan ahead to have a small package of goodies waiting at his or her destination.
- *Host a homecoming.* Invite the returning teen to share his or her experiences with your group. Look at the photos and listen to the stories of how God worked in and through your young friend's life.

—Karen H. Whiting

73
Royalty for a Day

It was like being royalty for a day! We were home on furlough, and a member of a small group that had adopted us as their special missionaries was treating us to an evening out. We started with dinner in a lovely restaurant, then attended a local theater production.

This was not the first time the small group had reached out to us, nor did they limit their outreach to when we were on furlough. When they were using a particular book as the focus for their studies, they sent us a copy to enjoy along with them. Each month, a group member wrote us or organized a joint letter about the day-to-day happenings of their families.

Many in overseas Christian work feel like we did—cut off, forgotten, and looked upon as strange creatures who were so heavenly minded we would never enjoy attending a football game, listening to classical music, or reading anything but the Bible.

This group, in adopting us, took the time and trouble to get to know who we really are. At potluck dinners together, we were encouraged to share not only what we were doing overseas but our personal and ministry challenges. In turn, the group members shared their lives with us. Even though the group has now disbursed, we continue to stay in touch with several of them and still feel like adopted members of a special family.

Is there a Christian worker your small group could spoil a bit?

—Jack Henderson

Outreach

Evangelism

74
Seeking Lost Sheep

Sometimes a small group will identify itself by saying: "We're a shepherding group, not an evangelistic group." Is it right to concentrate solely on the needs of your own group?

> "This is what the Sovereign LORD says: 'Woe to the shepherds of Israel who only take care of themselves! Should not shepherds take care of the flock? . . . You have not strengthened the weak or healed the sick or bound up the injured. You have not brought back the strays or searched for the lost. . . . My sheep wandered over all the mountains and on every high hill. They were scattered over the whole earth, and no one searched or looked for them.'"
>
> —EZEKIEL 34:2,4,6

This passage confirmed for me that part of the job of a shepherd is taking care of the flock. But another role is seeking the lost. Shepherding and evangelism are not competing or contrasting values. The good shepherd was extremely evangelistic. Seeking the lost is part of shepherding.

The small-group leader can be an evangelistic shepherd by helping his or her "flock" search for lost sheep.

- *Model concern for the unsaved.* Make friendship evangelism a personal priority. Eat lunch with unbelieving coworkers. Take on a hobby that puts you in contact with nonChristians. Throw a block party for your neighbors. As you develop relationships and start sharing your faith with others, talk about your experiences with your small group.

- *Pray for the lost.* In your small-group meetings, make a priority of praying for unsaved friends and neighbors. Ask each person to write the names of unsaved friends on index cards, and pray as a group for those people. Encourage members to take cards home and pray during the week.

- *Serve together.* Express God's love to people in your community by serving them as a group. Steve Sjogren's book *Conspiracy of Kindness* and Servant Evangelism's web site (www.kindness.com) have many good ideas.

- *Welcome others.* Look for ways to invite unsaved friends to small-group activities. Hold barbecues and other open events where they will feel comfortable.

—MICHAEL C. MACK

75
Groups for Truth Seekers

Over the years I've tried several ideas for generating Bible-based discussions with unchurched friends and associates in a small-group setting. Here are three formats that have resulted in good discussions and additional opportunities to talk about my faith. (As you invite people into your home, explain in advance the format for the evening, and set—and stick to—a time frame that's convenient for all.)

- *Confronting the headlines.* Spiritual or "religious" issues—such as heaven, hell, divine inspiration of Scripture, angels, healing, cults, and "the historical Jesus"—regularly make the front cover of major magazines such as *Time, Newsweek,* and *U.S. News & World Report.* I invited neighbors, coworkers, and a few others to a one-night discussion of such issues. My primary goal was to draw out their questions and perspectives without being judgmental or condescending.
- *To create a "safe" environment,* I assured group members that they could pass on any question and just listen to what others had to say. I tried to keep my initial questions open-ended, requiring more than a yes or no answer. I prepared some questions ahead of time—a "tickler" list to rely on if the conversation bogged down. But as much as possible, I encouraged participants to ask questions of their own.
- *I tried to stay away from "Christianese"*—words that would have meaning only to me. At the end of the first discussion, a number of people were excited about continuing, so we met for several weeks. One person brought friends to one of our discussions.
- *Searching the scriptures. The Message,* a paraphrase of the Bible by Eugene H. Peterson, is contemporary and reads somewhat like a novel because it does not have verse numbers. I like using it with nonChristians. I studied on my own to find key Scriptures that speak to contemporary issues such as honesty, integrity, and fear. Eventually I narrowed down the Scriptures

to two or three per issue. I didn't want to overwhelm people with too many verses, and I tried to stay away from passages where the meaning is hidden or demands significant Bible knowledge to discern. During our discussion, I found it helpful to refer to the Scriptures by page number and line on the page. My questions were simple: What do you think is being said here? Does this passage say anything to you personally? If so, what? In such a group, feel free to share your own perspectives but allow others to go first if they will. At the end of the first discussion, I asked who would like to meet again. Some did. Two of those who returned also visited our church.

- *Movies with a message.* Another simple way to reach out to neighbors is with videos. Choose movies people have already seen or read about. Rather than watch the entire video together, I isolated a small section (no more than seven or eight minutes), and we discussed personal, relational, and other values it represented. It was fairly easy to tie the discussion to some thought-provoking Scriptures. I find it works best if I don't whip out my thick study Bible or a long list of Scriptures. Instead, I quote in contemporary language or accurately paraphrase a Scripture I have memorized (or that has significantly impacted me). Some video clips I use are from
  It's a Wonderful Life
  Simon Birch
  What Dreams May Come
  Sister Act
  Michael
  City of Angels
  Ever After
  Armageddon

—Thom Corrigan

76
Acting Out

Most of us have encountered opportunities to speak about Christ's good news to relatives, neighbors, coworkers, and hurting people. But we don't always have the presence of mind to come up with the right words. We end up kicking ourselves for letting an open door slam in our faces because we were unprepared.

A few friends and I began role-playing what we might say in different witnessing situations. We know the Holy Spirit is the one who opens a heart for Christ, but role-playing has helped us be ready when God leads us to speak.

Evangelism role-playing is a great activity for small groups. Here are some scenarios to start with. Divide your group into twos or threes and start practicing.

- A coworker is dying of cancer. I want to talk to him about eternal life, but I'm not sure how to work it into a conversation.
- We're flying home for Christmas. Our relatives already think we're overzealous cult members. We're paranoid about speaking of our faith.
- A coworker just found out she's pregnant. She is considering an abortion, yet I sense she doesn't really want to do that. Now might be a perfect time to talk to her about Jesus.
- A two-year-old boy in our neighborhood is on life support after falling into his family's pool. I'm going to the hospital to visit this family. They don't go to church; I'm not sure what their beliefs are about God. I want to offer love and hope.
- My neighbor and I often talk for a few minutes when we get the mail or pick up our newspapers. Lately I've felt this overwhelming desire to speak with him about the Lord. But I'm afraid I might offend him, and he'll want nothing more to do with me.
- I spot a sad-looking elderly gentleman sitting on a bench at the mall. My first impulse is to talk to him about Jesus. But I have no idea how to approach a stranger and start a conversation.

Role-playing with your small-group members will prepare you to give an answer when people ask about the hope in you (see 1 Peter 3:15).

—Rhonda Reese

77
Ready for Action

Your small group can be a place where believers prepare themselves for witnessing opportunities. Try some of these ideas to encourage and equip yourselves for evangelism.

- *Tag team witnessing.* Appoint a member of your group who is good at presenting either side of an argument to role-play the unbeliever. A group member tries to witness to this "nonChristian." If he or she gets stumped, another group member who thinks he has the answer can "tag" the witness and take over.

- *Translator.* Brainstorm a list of words that Christians use but that nonChristians would either misunderstand or not know at all. Record your answers on a large flip-chart or marker board. Now ask group members to write a one-page explanation of how to become a Christian—without using any of these words. Expect a struggle as you try to communicate spiritual truth in everyday language. Read your compositions aloud and discuss how you can make your explanations even easier to understand.

- *Postal service.* Ask each group member to write a letter to a fictional friend or relative who thinks he or she is a religious person. Explain what it means to be a Christian. Address questions such as, Why is being a moral person not enough? Why do some Christians live immoral lives? Are Christians too narrow-minded? What difference does Jesus make in your life? Read and discuss your letters.

- *Autobiography.* Write two-page descriptions of what led each of you to become Christians. What people, books, events, and so on influenced you? What barriers did you face? What doubts? How did your life change after you met Christ? Discuss your stories as a group. Try to anticipate questions that nonChristians would ask.

—JOHN GREEN

78
In Our Own Backyards

Last summer, our small group didn't study the Bible. We didn't pray much together either. And worship was definitely out in our group. Instead, we had picnics, played *Pictionary* in the backyard, washed cars, babysat, threw a party, and attended a few others.

We began planning these summer activities when our group started meeting the previous fall. The idea was to invite our neighbors to join in our fun so we could get to know them better. We also did service projects in the neighbor-hood—nonthreatening things like providing free babysitting for young couples so they could enjoy a night on the town.

This fall, we began the *Building Your Marriage* study by Dennis Rainey, part of the FAMILY LIFE HOMEBUILDERS COUPLES SERIES (Gospel Light). We invited our newfound neighborhood friends to join us. Later, after they've had a chance to see that the Bible is relevant to real life, we'll study the Gospel of John with them.

By then, we hope our group will have grown. And we pray the kingdom will grow, too, as these neighbors meet Jesus—first through our lives and actions, then through a study of a relevant topic like marriage, then through studying the Bible.

By the way, our group has resumed praying—for each other and for people we've met in the neighborhood who don't yet know Jesus. We're worshiping, too, offering ourselves as living sacrifices to people so they may see God through us (see Romans 12:1).

Some Christians went on short-term missionary trips to places all over the world last summer. Our group took the gospel to people in our own backyard—literally.

—MICHAEL C. MACK

Outreach

Serving

79
Selected Saints

We started a "Saint of the Week" club. Our group prayerfully selects one saint from our church—someone in leadership, a teenager, senior citizen, shut-in, and so on. During our prayer time, we pray for that person or family. Then we write a few sentences on a note card to tell that person how much we appreciate him and his service to the church and how important he is to God. We receive many encouraging comments from the recipients of our notes. We see this as a way to build up the Body of Christ.

—Linda Long

80
Members with a Mission

Our cell group wanted to be doers, and not just hearers, of the Word.

So one Tuesday night, we drove to the nearby gospel mission in Kalamazoo, Michigan, to visit with the residents. (We'd received permission from the mission administrators first.) We prayed that they would experience Jesus' love for them through us.

Most of the people we met were dealing with drug and alcohol problems. All of them were lonely. We spent the evening just talking to them individually or in small clusters. We asked them for prayer requests (they had many) and assured them that our whole church would be praying for them. On the way home, we talked about what it was like to step out of our comfort zones to visit the mission and what we learned from the experience.

We've been back a couple of times since then. This is such a simple form of ministry, yet it means a lot to lonely, struggling people. Try it with a mission, nursing home, or hospital near you.

—Steve Bensinger

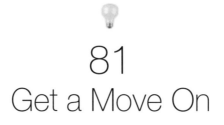

81
Get a Move On

When someone in our church needs to move, our small group offers our services. We have found that helping people move can be a great testimony to both old and new neighbors. People who don't know Jesus are always impressed that we willingly give our time to help someone settle into a new home. In our small, mobile church, we've assisted in about five moves a year.

We don't do all the work ourselves; we announce moves and recruit volunteers from the congregation. Anyone can help; there are always small things to be carried. We've learned that certain people gravitate toward this ministry, and we call them specifically.

If your church is large, your small group might want to focus on a specific segment, such as single moms or the elderly. You may decide that you can only handle a couple of moves a year. However you choose to set up your ministry, here are our suggestions for making the move work.

Before the Move
- The person moving is responsible for renting and picking up the truck.
- Ask the person moving to have everything packed before you arrive (except cleaning supplies). Have them label boxes according to the room they will go into.
- If there are small children in the household, arrange for a church member to care for them away from the moving site.

Moving Day
- When you arrive at the house, spend a few minutes planning what needs to be loaded onto the truck first. Designate someone with a good eye for space and packing to remain in the van and coordinate the loading.
- As rooms are emptied, ask volunteers to begin cleaning. We usually dust walls, clean floors, wipe out cabinets, and clean bathrooms. This service is probably appreciated the most.
- As soon as the beds are unloaded at the new home, recruit someone to reassemble them and make them up with fresh linens. When exhaustion hits, the newly moved will be grateful you took care of this chore.

—Carol R. Cool

82
What Is a Pastor?

One small-group study that is always helpful—and also eye-opening—is a survey of what the Bible says a pastor is to be and do. Because it is difficult for pastors to preach on this issue without appearing self-seeking, a small group is an ideal place to explore this topic (we start with 1 and 2 Timothy). Many church members have no idea what Scripture says a pastor's job really is. Their often unrealistic expectations are usually based on traditions, experiences with previous pastors, or their own agendas rather than on biblical principles. Once people have a better understanding of how their pastor should be investing his or her time, energy, and resources, they also have a better understanding of what they are called to do.

—NOELLE SCHLECHTY

83
Students in Cyberspace

Many young people have e-mail addresses at college. Our small group "adopts" a student from our church and e-mails him or her at least once a week. We share church news, happenings around town, and Scripture. We let the student know he or she is missed and prayed for. Our cyberspace is humming with exhilarating two-way conversations.

—GAIL A. BRADFORD

84
Pamper Your Pastor

For several years now, October has been designated Clergy Appreciation Month. While pastors deserve a month of special honor, why not also spread expressions of thanks throughout the year?

In early October, send a note to the pastor saying, "Our small group wants you to know that we appreciate you. However, we don't believe we can express our gratitude adequately in one month. Therefore, we are extending the benefits of Clergy Appreciation Month. You will hear from one member of our group each month during the coming year." Ask group members to sign up for their preferred month. Then schedule some of the following ideas—and brainstorm more of your own.

- *Plan a work project.* Does the pastor have a home-improvement project your group could tackle? Maybe the house needs painting or the roof needs repairs. Would the family enjoy a vegetable garden? Anything that will improve your pastor's quality of life would be welcome. Give your pastor's family a break from chores: window washing, lawn care, housecleaning, and so on. Combine a carry-in dinner with the work project.
- *Sponsor a retreat.* Finance a trip for husband and wife to get away for renewal. Arrange for childcare, if needed, so the parents can enjoy a complete break.
- *Provide monthly treats.* Give a gift subscription to a magazine the pastor would enjoy. Place an order for fruit, nuts, or other delicacies to be delivered monthly.
- *Coordinate with other groups.* To avoid duplication of efforts, learn what other groups in your church may be doing for your pastor. If you know of a need that would be more costly or more work intensive than your group can manage, pool resources with another group. This approach also works well when you have more than one pastor on staff.

—Esther M. Bailey

85
Love by the Month

Our small group—all moms—thrived on park dates, poolside fellowship, the occasional girls' night out, and other bonding activities. After a while, however, we experienced a greater desire: We wanted to give a touch of love to those who needed it. We discovered that acts of charity brought us closer to each other and, even more important, humbled us before God's throne of grace. Following is a year's worth of ideas for your group.

- *January.* Look for a family in need because of job loss, medical crisis, or other circumstances. Bring them dinner and encouragement one night.
- *February.* Bake or buy valentine cookies (with or without sugar), and take them to a convalescent home. Call ahead for an appointment, and make sure to set aside plenty of time to visit.
- *March.* Throw a baby shower for the local crisis pregnancy center.
- *April.* Give the gift of spring cleaning or house repairs to an elderly friend.
- *May.* Plant a vegetable garden, and make a list of local nonprofit food organizations that will receive your bounty at harvest time. Schedule delivery with these groups for sometime in the summer.
- *June.* Volunteer to handle one area—such as snacks, games, or story time—for a vacation Bible school outreach.
- *July.* Hold a backyard barbecue and invite the neighbors. Groups that meet in a church can throw an open house for neighboring businesses or residents.
- *August.* Adopt a missionary. Pray at each meeting this month for a missionary (and family, if applicable). Mail them a box of treats such as American magazines, gourmet chocolates, and toiletries. Let them know your group has prayed for them all month long.
- *September.* Drop off a huge box of doughnuts to the teachers' lounge at a local school. Leave a note telling the faculty members you are praying they will have a fantastic year.
- *October.* No tricks, just treats! Purchase high-quality sweets, label them with personal notes such as "Jesus loves you" or a Scripture verse, and deliver them to the neighborhood kids.
- *November.* Volunteer to serve dinner at a local rescue mission the weekend after Thanksgiving, once all the holiday helpers have gone home.
- *December.* Don Santa hats, and deliver to needy families boxes of nonperishable food and gifts collected by your church.

—Julie Marie Carobini

86
Secret Service

Inspired by Matthew 6:3, our group makes secret deliveries of groceries, flowers, notes, and other niceties to unsuspecting recipients. With each delivery we leave a card illustrated with the outline of a hand; our group's pseudonym, "The Right Hand"; and a verse that would best minister to that person's situation. Remember, "But when you give to the needy, do not let your left hand know what your right hand is doing, so that your giving may be in secret" (see Matthew 6:3-4).

We sometimes leave the gifts on the doorstep and then run off, like kids playing a prank. Other times, we have the goods delivered by a third party to the person's home or office. Whatever method we use, we always enjoy the opportunity to "proclaim in humility the wonders He has done" and be a blessing for others.

—Name Withheld

Holidays

87
New Year, New Goals

The new year is the perfect time for small-group goal setting. Discuss the upcoming year together. Brainstorm about what you'd like to accomplish together. Identify four to five goals your group can adopt. Make sure each is ownable, measurable, and achievable. Then write them down so each member has a copy.

Here are some possible small-group objectives to stimulate your brainstorming.

- *Scripture memory.* Would your group like to memorize portions of the Bible? Set up a system to hold one another accountable. Some groups have learned large chunks together, such as the Sermon on the Mount or Philippians.

- *Prayer.* Are there people your group would like to pray for, but haven't? For example, you might want to pray for an unreached people group, your neighborhood, or your pastor. Perhaps you can pray about group members' personal concerns on a deeper level.

- *Vulnerability.* How might you be more open and honest with each other in the year ahead? Do you need to adopt new practices to increase transparency, such as stricter confidentiality or more sharing time?

- *Service.* How many service projects do you want to do as a group this year? Set a goal, brainstorm possibilities, then get cracking!

- *Bible.* Does your group desire greater clarity about doctrinal issues or certain portions of Scripture? If so, identify possible resources and start studying.

- *Worship.* Are there ways your group can grow in your ability to worship God? How might you introduce new worship dynamics into regular group meetings? Perhaps you could attend another denomination's worship service to observe a different worship style.

- *Fun.* Identify two or three fun activities to enjoy this year. Meet at a restaurant for breakfast on a Saturday morning. Go river rafting. How about a group camping trip? Plan your activities now so you'll have a better chance of actually doing them.

The goals you set today pave the way to a rewarding and spiritually rich year.

—KEITH D. WRIGHT

88
A Time of Seeking

Close out the old year and bring in the new with a Time of Seeking in your small group. Here's how it works.

Gather in a place large enough for group members to spread out. To prepare hearts to hear from God, spend a short time in corporate worship.

Hand out and go over the following format for spending the next hour alone with God. Don't treat this as an assignment but rather as a guide; some members of your group may already have a clear idea of how to spend an hour in prayer.

- *A time of laying down concerns* (20 minutes). "Cast all your anxiety on him because he cares for you" (1 Peter 5:7). If you're entering this Time of Seeking with a lot of concerns, start by listing them. Jot down everything that concerns you, no matter how small. One by one, go through your list. If you can't do anything about the concern, bring it before the Lord in prayer. If you can do something about it, spend time praying about it, and then write down the action you need to take on a "to do list." Conclude this time by committing all of your concerns to the Lord.

- *A time of reflection* (20 minutes). "I will remember the deeds of the LORD; yes, I will remember your miracles of long ago" (Psalm 77:11). Think over the events of the past year. On one page make a list of struggles and failures in the past year. One by one, go through each item on the list. Confess your sins to the Lord. Ask for His forgiveness and thank Him for an opportunity to start fresh. On another page make a list of blessings and successes from the past year. Thank and praise God for His goodness in your life last year.

- *A time of looking forward* (20 minutes). "'For I know the plans I have for you,' declares the LORD, 'plans to prosper you and not to harm you, plans to give you hope and a future'" (Jeremiah 29:11). Ask God what He would like to accomplish in and through you in the next year. You might want to consider the following areas: spiritual life, family life, ministry, career, and finances. Take one area at a time and wait on God, asking Him to reveal His plans for your life. Jot down your thoughts as they come to you. Spend time praying about each area.

Conclude this hour by thanking God for His forgiveness, His provision in the past, and His plans for your future. After the individual prayer time concludes, gather for corporate communion. Conclude by giving people an opportunity to share about their hour in prayer.

—Rebecca Livermore

89
A Valentine's Day Exercise

Devote one of your February small-group meetings to focusing on God's love for you.

Imagine Him sending you a valentine or love letter. According to Deuteronomy 33:12; Epheseans 5:1; and Colossians 3:12, how might He address you?

Imagine Him expressing His love for you with words like those you'll find in these verses: Isaiah 43:4; Isaiah 62:3; Jeremiah 31:3; and Zephaniah 3:17.

Have each person cut a large heart from a sheet of red or pink construction paper. Spend the next 10 to 15 minutes writing individual love letters to God on your paper "valentines." Close by thanking God in sentence prayers for His intimate, personal love.

—Author unknown

90
P.S. I Love You

Each February, with the approach of Valentine's Day, our small-group members make homemade valentines. The activity itself is fun because we get to make a big mess with glue, crayons, markers, construction paper, glitter, doilies, sequins, and so on. What has made our approach unique is that each year we choose a different category of person to send a valentine to. So far, we've made valentines for our parents, grandparents, siblings, pastors, and mentors. After we make our cards, we spend time relating what positive influence our "valentine" has had in our lives, then we pray for that person.

—Sue Kline

91
Easter Small-Group Style

Small groups are wonderful places to celebrate Easter. Choose one or two of these ideas to try this year.

- Ask an aspiring actor in your group to read a selection from Max Lucado's *No Wonder They Call Him the Savior* or *Six Hours One Friday* or another favorite devotional work that focuses on the events of Holy Week.
- Listen to classical music written for Easter, such as John Rutter's *Requiem*, Bach's *St. Matthew Passion* or *Easter Oratio*, or Mozart's *Requiem*. If possible, attend together a local performance of one of these works. Gather at someone's home afterward for dessert and coffee, and talk about how the music enriched your understanding of Easter.
- Celebrate Passover. Many churches now include "Christ in the Passover" seder meals among their Easter activities. Find one near you and attend together.
- Prepare together one or more of the traditional foods associated with Easter. Ask one group member to research the meaning behind traditions such as coloring eggs, preparing Easter bread or hot cross buns, and so on. Some foods and traditions are rooted in pagan spring rites, but talk about how you can "redeem" them and give them spiritual significance.
- Pitch in and purchase Easter lilies or other flowers of the season, then deliver them to nursing homes, homeless shelters, halfway houses, soup kitchens, and other places that will benefit from a touch of beauty.

—Sue Kline

92
Robed in Righteousness

To remind your small-group members of Christ's once-and-for-all sacrifice on the cross this Easter, try this activity. Fashion a cross from planks, and stand it upright in a large flowerpot at the center of the room. After praying together, ask each team member to spend 15 minutes "confessing" sins by writing them individually on index cards. Next, direct members to fold the paper and then attach it to the cross with a staple gun or thumbtacks. After the cards are all attached, read aloud several Scripture passages dealing with Christ's Passion, His forgiveness of our sins, and our righteousness in Him. Finish by reading Isaiah 61:10: "My soul shall be joyful in my God; For He has clothed me with the garments of salvation, He has covered me with the robe of righteousness" (NKJV). As this verse is read, cover the cross with a length of beautiful fabric. Join hands around the cross, and thank God together for His redemption.

—RICHARD HURST

93
Small Group Seder

Each year our small group observes a Christian Passover. The evening has become a valued and much anticipated tradition as it brings to life the symbols and fulfillment of the Passover.

Years ago, while studying Exodus, I decided to prepare a Passover dinner for my family. That first year our celebration was very basic. I had no idea where to start except with the story itself in Exodus 12. I planned the meal around lamb and unleavened bread, adding some other dishes to make it a complete dinner.

That night, my husband took a bowl of water and a branch from a bush onto the front porch. We all watched him paint the doorframe as he explained the protection this "blood" offered the Israelites. We then discussed the Passover events and the symbols of the meal while we ate. We compared them to the events of Jesus' last Passover with His disciples and talked about Jesus as our Passover lamb.

The next year, I called a local rabbi to ask about the foods and symbols in a traditional Jewish Passover meal. Over the years, as we invited friends to join us, we refined our celebration further. Soon our small group got involved. Some explored the Jewish Passover service and culled messianic Passover resources to produce a script for our celebration; others found recipes for some of the traditional foods. It has now become a yearly tradition as different families host the group. We often invite a family or two from outside our church, giving us a great opportunity to explain the biblical story.

—MONEMA STEPHENS

94
Make a Note of It

Writing thank-you notes is a drag, right? Not if you turn this "chore" into a small-group activity. As Thanksgiving approaches, replace your usual meeting agenda with a night of written thanksgiving. Ask every person to bring five blank note cards and envelopes. When you first arrive, brainstorm people you want to thank as a small group: your pastor, your worship leader, your elders and deacons, missionaries you help support, a Sunday school teacher, and so on. Divvy up your brainstorming list so that each person will write three thank-you notes. After that's done, instruct group members to use their fourth blank note to write a word of thanks to the person on their left. Now, people should use their last blank note to write their thanks to God. Encourage group members to carry this thank-you note to God in their Bibles as a reminder to more frequently "come before him with thanksgiving" (Psalm 95:2).

—SUE KLINE

95
A Meal with Meaning

Our group looks forward each year to our Thanksgiving progressive dinner. Normally we go to three different homes for the traditional food and fellowship. However, last year my wife and I surprised everyone with a "Progressive Prayer Dinner."

In the first home, instead of warming up to tasty appetizers, we stood around a small pot of very thin chicken broth and talked about the millions of poor among us. We prayed for the needs of those who continue in physical, emotional, and spiritual poverty.

Our next stop is usually the soup and salad course. Instead, we all went to a garage where we gathered on the concrete floor next to a bowl of rice. The purpose of this stop was to highlight the plight of the thousands of brothers and sisters in

Christ who, at that particular moment, were quietly suffering imprisonment, torture, or even death for His name's sake. We prayed about the needs of the persecuted Christians and asked God to help us remember to pray for them regularly.

Finally, we moved on to our home for an elaborate turkey dinner with all the trimmings. In light of the previous stops, our talk centered on God's abundant, undeserved provision and the extent that He has blessed our country. We thanked Him for His mercy and grace in our lives, and we asked Him to help us become better stewards of His blessings.

Our progressive prayer dinner was a big hit, though sobering. Reflecting on His goodness was humbling and has changed the way we think about Thanksgiving.

—RICK McKIBBEN

96
The ABCs of Thankfulness

During the Thanksgiving season, use this idea to help your group members express gratitude. Distribute lined paper and pencils to everyone in your group. Ask them to write the words "Thank you, God, for . . . " at the top of the paper. Down the left margin of the paper, they should write the letters of the alphabet, one per line.

Instruct the members to spend 15 minutes listing things they are grateful for in the space next to each letter. Remind them to consider the various ways God blesses us: spiritually, physically, mentally, emotionally, materially, and relationally. Try to record at least one blessing for each letter.

At the end of the time limit, ask the group members to share some of their blessings as you go through the alphabet. Encourage them to save their lists as reminders of God's goodness or for use in personal devotions. For fun, you might have people add the number of blessings they listed and give a prize to the one who recorded the most. End the game with prayers of thanksgiving, using your lists for inspiration.

—LORRAINE ESPINOSA

97
Christmas Parties
That Travel

Before you schedule your usual small-group Christmas party, think about doing something different this year—such as taking your party on the road. How?

- *Cheer for children.* Load up on children's Christmas books, and "invade" (with permission) the pediatric ward of your local hospital. Read to the kids and distribute holiday-colored balloons, candy canes, inexpensive toys (yo-yos, crayons, and so on). If your group talents permit it, lead the children in singing Christmas songs, or present an age-appropriate skit for their entertainment.
- *Bake-a-thon.* Gather at the home of the group member with the biggest kitchen, and spend the day baking homemade bread for a homeless shelter or soup kitchen. Stick to hearty, whole-grain loaves that will pack plenty of nutritional punch. Make a loaf or two to enjoy on the spot as well.
- *Flower power.* Take small poinsettias to nursing-home residents. Spread out, spend time talking to people one on one, and ask them to tell you what Christmas was like in their youth. The gift of your time and listening ear may be the most precious gift they receive at Christmas.
- *Christmas crafts.* Is your group crafty? One group, whose members were skilled in knitting and crocheting, dedicated one evening a week for four weeks to making mittens, scarves, hats, and socks. Homeless shelters, crisis pregnancy centers, and shelters for battered women appreciate such gifts.
- *Holiday hammers.* If you live in a mild climate and if Habitat for Humanity is building a home near you, replace your Christmas party with a work day at a Habitat project. Brighten the day for other volunteers by wearing holiday duds and bringing a boom box and Christmas tapes. Bring enough Christmas fare to fuel yourselves and your coworkers.
- *Church elves.* Volunteer as a group to help with one of your church's seasonal outreach projects, such as delivering presents for Project Angel Tree, which collects and distributes gifts to the children of prisoners.

The Christmas season is insanely busy for most of us. But before you groan at the thought of adding one of these activities to your calendar, remember that these outreach projects would replace your regular Christmas party. You're not taking on more—you're just taking your party on the road.

—SUE KLINE

Summer

98
Poolside Proverbs

Small groups often take a hiatus in the summer while members travel or spend extra time with family. This year, use that break to explore the wisdom of Proverbs; then discuss your findings when you reconvene.

Ask members to read one chapter of Proverbs twice each day. At the morning reading, note the verses that have special meaning. Read the same chapter again in the evening to see if another passage jumps out, or if the earlier verses have acquired additional significance.

When you meet again at the end of the summer break, ask each member to name the five verses that had the most impact and explain why they were significant.

When our group did this, we found everyone was moved by different verses. One young man spoke very poignantly about how he had been admonished in his reading. One zealous member had used four different versions of the Bible for her study. Our entire group found this to be a rewarding and enlightening assignment.

—Betty Thompson

99
Keeping in Touch

Many small groups take a summer break. Now is the time to plan how you'll stay in touch during the months you aren't meeting. Which of these ideas might work for your group?

- Set up a prayer chain that will keep you linked together through intercession.
- Before you break for the summer, set a date and place for a mid-summer potluck picnic or cookout.
- Plan a weekend camping trip for the entire group.
- Select a book (preferably a skinny one) that each person commits to read

over the summer. When you gather in the fall, spend your first meeting discussing what you learned.

- Discuss in May what summer projects you hope to accomplish (reroof the house, can your own vegetables, build a sandbox for the kids, and so on). How can you team up and help each other reach your goals?
- Make a date to have brunch together after church on the first Sunday of June, July, and August.

—AUTHOR UNKNOWN

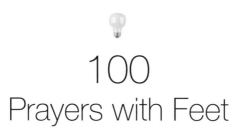

100
Prayers with Feet

When the days get longer and the air gets balmier, some small groups start winding down toward a summer break. Instead of losing touch with each other for three months, set up a schedule to walk together with various small-group members. But not just to walk. Take turns walking in each other's neighborhoods and praying for the families there.

Here's how it works. Before your last meeting of the spring, decide on a day (or evening) of the week that will be your summer "prayer walk" time—for whomever is available. Let's assume that your group members live in four different neighborhoods throughout your city or town. Assign a neighborhood to each week. For example, week one you will walk in Arlington Heights where Jack and Linda live. Week two you will walk in Rock Valley where Sam lives. And so on. Once you gather at the specified time and place, split into pairs. As you walk through the assigned neighborhood, pray for the people who live there. Ask God to work in their hearts through His Spirit so they will hunger for Him. Ask Him to open doors so the small-group members who live in that neighborhood will have opportunities to reach out in love to neighbors and speak to them of how important Christ is in their lives. Pray for specific needs you might know about through your small-group members.

At first, this may seem awkward and difficult. In time, you'll become more comfortable and will sense God's Spirit prompting your prayers. By fall, when your group starts meeting again, you may be amazed at how God is working in your neighborhoods through your prayers.

—SUE KLINE

101
School's Out

Our small group for moms faced a dilemma: What should we do with our kids while we met during the summer? Our solution: Bring the kids along and make them the focus of the meeting. We have done this for the last three summers. It has the advantage of providing continuing fellowship for the moms (we would go crazy without some adult conversation), as well as giving a "program" for the kids one morning a week. We get a chance to have some spiritual input into our children's lives; we also use the gathering as an opportunity to invite our nonChristian friends.

If this sounds appropriate for your group, we offer this advice from our experience.

- *Divide and conquer.* Don't let one mom do it all. Rotate the meeting place from house to house. The mother who offers her house should not provide snacks, do the teaching, or plan activities—picking up all those toys before and after the meeting is enough!
- *Serve suitable snacks.* Forget the herbal tea and scones. Minister to your kids by making the food fun for them.
- *Teach kid-style.* Keep it simple and short. Use visual aids such as puppets or flannelboards, or act out a story with your children's dolls and stuffed animals. If your creative juices have run dry by the end of the school year, check your Christian bookstore for materials. You can also search for "children's ministry resources" on the Internet.
- *Open up.* Parents who would never go to a church will come with their children to a "kids' thing." Tell them up front that a Bible story will be part of the program. (And pray!) The children's story can be an inoffensive way to share the gospel with parents. Several parents who have come to our summer meetings have later visited our Bible studies.

We are always glad to get back to our regular small-group meetings at the end of the summer. However, the change of pace refreshes us, keeps us in touch, serves our summer needs, and gives us a chance to reach out to other moms. Last summer, as one mother shared the story of Jesus' disciples in the boat during the storm—complete with group participation on the wind, rain, thunder, and lightning—another mom, enthralled, commented, "We should do our Bible studies like this!"

—Laura Turner De Gomez

LOOKING FOR YOUR NEXT BIBLE STUDY?

Beating Busyness
by Adam Holz • 1-57683-155-8

Despite technological advances and enhanced communication, our "to do" lists are longer than ever. Identify and tackle stressful issues in your life through articles, questions, quotes, Scripture, and related exercises. Based on excerpts from top *Discipleship Journal* articles, this study will challenge you to deal effectively with busyness.

Building Better Relationships
by Susan Nikaido • 1-57683-167-1

Based on top *Discipleship Journal* articles, this Bible study offers a wealth of insight to help you develop deeper vulnerability, sensitivity, and love in all your relationships—at work, home, or anywhere.

Growing Deeper with God
by Susan Nikaido • 1-57683-153-1

Discover how you can become an intimate friend of God. Learn to focus on Him and reorder your priorities as you interact with God personally. Begin to experience the kind of closeness with God that your heart longs for.

Redeeming Failure
by Michael M. Smith • 1-57683-164-7

Does failure frighten you? Get beyond its paralyzing effects and learn how failure can be a necessary discipline to grow in Christ. For growing or mature believers, this *Discipleship Journal* Bible study is designed to help you develop a deeper relationship with God.

TRY ONE OF THESE GREAT STUDIES FROM
 Discipleship Journal.®

Becoming More Like Jesus
by Michael M. Smith • 1-57683-156-6

Becoming like Jesus is a process, not learning a list of rules. Based on excerpts from top *Discipleship Journal* articles, this study will develop His character in you as you evaluate your life, understand Jesus' teachings on character, and live them out.

Following God in Tough Times
by Michael M. Smith • 1-57683-157-4

Even when we feel imprisoned by life's difficult circumstances, God gives us freedom to choose how we'll respond. Learn how to accept and gain perspective on tough times as you move from survival to service.

Nurturing a Passion for Prayer
by Michael M. Smith • 1-57683-165-5

Is your experience with prayer less than passionate communication with God? Change your attitude toward prayer. The staff of *Discipleship Journal* designed this study to help you discover intimate interaction with the heavenly Father.

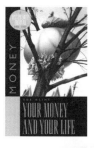

Your Money and Your Life
by Sue Kline • 1-57683-166-3

Discover how to handle your finances and your possessions—whether many or few—in a way that leaves you free to find true satisfaction, generosity, and contentment with what God has given you.

 Discipleship Journal BOOKS

 NAVPRESS®
BRINGING TRUTH TO LIFE

www.discipleshipjournal.com   www.navpress.com

TRY STUDYING THE BIBLE IN A NEW WAY.

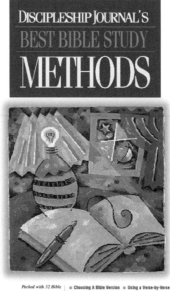